D0149477

How *to*

USE
PROBLEM-BASED
LEARNING
IN THE
CLASSROOM

Robert Delisle

Association for Supervision and Curriculum Development
Alexandria, Virginia USA

Association for Supervision and Curriculum Development
1250 N. Pitt Street • Alexandria, Virginia 22314-1453 USA
Telephone: 1-800-933-2723 or 703-549-9110 • Fax: 703-299-8631
Web site: http://www.ascd.org • E-mail: member@ascd.org

Gene R. Carter, *Executive Director*
Michelle Terry, *Assistant Executive Director, Program Development*
Nancy Modrak, *Director, Publishing*
John O'Neil, *Acquisitions Editor*
Mark Goldberg, *Development Editor*
Julie Houtz, *Managing Editor of Books*
Margaret Oosterman, *Associate Editor*
René Bahrenfuss, *Copy Editor*
Gary Bloom, *Director, Design, Editorial, and Production Services*
Karen Monaco, *Senior Designer*
Tracey A. Smith, *Production Manager*
Dina Murray, *Production Assistant*
Cynthia Stock, *Desktop Publisher*

ASCD publications present a variety of viewpoints. The views
expressed or implied in this book should not be interpreted as
official positions of the Association.

Printed in the United States of America.

ASCD Stock No.: 197166
s12/97
ASCD member price: $10.95; nonmember price: $12.95

Library of Congress Cataloging-in-Publication Data

Delisle, Robert, 1937–
      How to use problem-based learning in the classroom / Robert
Delisle.
      p.   cm.
      Includes bibliographical references (p.).
      ISBN 0-87120-291-3 (pb)
      1. Problem-based learning.   I. Association for Supervision and
Curriculum Development.   II. Title.
LB1027.42.D45   1997
371.39—dc21   97-43045
                                                              CIP

01 00 99 98 97   5 4 3 2 1

How to Use Problem-Based Learning in the Classroom

Robert Delisle is Associate Professor of Education and Chair of the Department of Specialized Services in Education, Lehman College, City University of New York. He teaches in the graduate program in reading and may be reached at Lehman College, Bedford Park Boulevard West, Bronx, New York 10468.

Acknowledgments

I wish to thank Maxine Bleich and Phyllis McCabe for introducing me to problem-based learning (PBL); Howard Barrows, Anne Meyers, and Linda O'Brien for training me in PBL; the teachers and health professionals who have provided insights about the effective use of PBL; Sam Lubell, without whose contributions the manuscript would never have been completed; and finally Kathy Fountain and Virginia Snowden for their excellent technical skills.

Introduction

A
ll young children ask parents what could be called "why" questions. Why is the sky blue? Why do things fall down? And many times, children ask the same questions again a few days later. Even though children may not understand the answers, the questions themselves show that children are thinking about the world and developing habits of thought.

Similarly, in our adult lives, we build understanding largely through what we experience. We create meaning as much from efforts to answer our own questions as from what we read or hear. In that sense, it is often said that our greatest challenges become our greatest learning experiences.

That is the principle behind problem-based learning (PBL), a teaching technique that educates by presenting students with a situation that leads to a problem for them to solve. It is not just a way to get students to find a correct answer. Frequently the problems have no single "right" answer. Instead, students learn through the act of trying to solve the problem. They interpret the question, gather additional information, create possible solutions, evaluate options to find the best solutions, and then present their conclusions.

Originally designed for students at medical schools, problem-based learning made the leap to high school when the faculty of the BioPrep Program at the University of Alabama developed a high school program to increase the number of qualified minority and economically disadvantaged candidates accepted into medical schools. Although the faculty did not use PBL themselves, their research into effective science teaching convinced them that PBL could be adapted to high school science classes. Intrigued by the idea of introducing PBL to high schools, Howard Barrows, a pioneer in the development of PBL, agreed to work with the

Alabama schools to develop an anatomy/physiology course for high school juniors and seniors.

PBL took hold in Alabama schools affiliated with the Macy Foundation, though without the involvement of anyone at the Foundation. Affiliation with the Foundation meant that the schools already had a collaborative network in place, unlike many U.S. schools that aren't linked with an organization.

Word of this innovative teaching quickly spread among the teachers and school leaders working in other Macy-sponsored high school programs in Alabama and throughout the United States, even though PBL was not an official part of the Macy program. At conferences and professional exchanges, teachers and school leaders talked about Barrows's course and wanted to start their own anatomy/physiology courses using PBL. Making their own arrangements, these schools used Macy Foundation grant money to train each other. Macy money was used to support improvement of science instruction in high schools, with the idea of encouraging students to think about health careers. But there was no formal sustained relationship between the schools and Barrows other than the initial training in Alabama. On their own, the schools built PBL courses and developed problems, supporting each other.

This problem-based learning movement became more organized when a new nonprofit group, Ventures In Education (VIE), was formed to work with the Macy-sponsored high school programs and to expand their achievements into other schools nationwide. Macy schools were working on improving the performance of students in science, and VIE wanted to spread such efforts to other schools. VIE also wanted to encourage schools to use problem-based learning in a variety of curriculum areas.

In conferences held in 1990 and 1991, I was astonished at the number of school leaders who were practicing PBL by themselves and who were asking Ventures to help them further develop PBL across the disciplines to achieve the same high results with student performance and interest as in the anatomy/physiology course. Although this development was not part of the original Ventures In Education plan, it was impossible to ignore so many independent requests, which were soon echoed by Ventures staff members who had seen PBL in action. As a direct response to this teacher demand, PBL now has become integral to school improvement efforts, enabling schools to successfully place students from diverse backgrounds into more rigorous academic courses.

This book was written to make information about problem-based learning available to a greater number of teachers and to show them how to use these methods in their own classrooms. It shows how teachers can use PBL to replace passive listening and rote memorizing with active investigation, participation, and problem solving. This book serves as a guide to how classroom instructors can challenge their students by providing them with a structured opportunity to share information, prove their knowledge, and engage in independent learning. These skills are especially important for urban students who are too frequently stereotyped as unable or unwilling to achieve at high levels.

MAXINE BLEICH
President, Ventures In Education

1 What Is Problem-Based Learning?

> *To organize education so that natural active tenden-*
> *cies shall be fully enlisted in doing something, while*
> *seeing to it that the doing requires observation, the*
> *acquisition of information, and the use of a construc-*
> *tive imagination, is what needs to be done to improve*
> *social conditions.*
>
> *—Dewey 1916, 1944, p. 137*

All education involves either problem solving or preparation for problem solving. From mathematical calculations ("What does this equal?") to literary analysis ("What does this mean?") to scientific experiments ("Why and how does this happen?") to historical investigation ("What took place, and why did it occur that way?"), teachers show students how to answer questions and solve problems. When teachers and schools skip the problem-formulating stage—handing facts and procedures to students without giving them a chance to develop their own questions and investigate by themselves—students may memorize material but will not fully understand or be able to use it. Problem-based learning (PBL) provides a structure for discovery that helps students internalize learning and leads to greater comprehension.

Origin of Problem-Based Learning

The roots of problem-based learning can be traced to the progressive movement, especially to John Dewey's belief that teachers should teach by appealing to students' natural instincts to investigate and create. Dewey wrote that "the first approach to any subject in school, if thought is to be aroused and not words acquired, should be as unscholastic as possible"

(Dewey 1916, 1944, p. 154). For Dewey, students' experiences outside of school provide us with clues for how to adapt lessons based on what interests and engages them:

> Methods which are permanently successful in formal educa-
> tion . . . go back to the type of situation which causes reflec-
> tion out of school in ordinary life. They give pupils something
> to do, not something to learn; and the doing is of such a nature
> as to demand thinking, or the intentional noting of connec-
> tions; learning naturally results (Dewey 1916, 1944, p. 154).

More than 80 years after that was written, students still learn best by doing and by thinking through problems. Educators who use problem-based learning recognize that in the world outside of school, adults build their knowledge and skills as they solve a real problem or answer an important question—not through abstract exercises. In fact, PBL originally was developed for adults, to train doctors in how to approach and solve medical problems.

Traditionally, medical schools taught doctors by requiring them to memorize a great deal of information and then to apply the information in clinical situations. This straightforward approach did not fully prepare doctors for the real world where some patients might not be able to identify their symptoms or others might show multiple symptoms. Though students memorized basic medical information for tests in their courses, they did not know how to apply the information to real-life situations and so quickly forgot it.

Recognizing that Dewey's maxim held true for medical education, Howard Barrows, a physician and medical educator at McMaster University in Hamilton, Ontario, Canada, wanted to develop methods of instructing physicians that fostered their own capabilities for reflection outside of school in ordinary life. For Barrows, the ultimate objective of medical education was

> to produce doctors capable of managing health problems of
> those who seek their services, in a competent and humane
> way. To do this, the doctors . . . must have both knowledge
> and the ability to use it (Barrows 1985, p. 3).

While most medical schools focused on providing knowledge, Barrows thought this was just the first of three interdependent elements:

(1) an essential body of knowledge, (2) the ability to use . . . knowledge effectively in the evaluation and care of . . . patients' health problems, and (3) the ability to extend or improve that knowledge and to provide appropriate care for future problems which they must face (Barrows 1985, p. 3).

Medical schools generally agreed on the content that should be taught; how this material should be learned remained an issue. Barrows developed problem-based learning to

allow [medical] students to integrate, use, and reuse newly learned information in the context of patients' problems; the symptoms, signs, laboratory data, course of illness, etc., provide cues for retrieval in the clinical context (Barrows 1985, p. 5).

This led to his first educational objective for PBL:

The medical students we educate must acquire basic science knowledge that is better retained, retrieved, and later used in the clinical context (Barrows 1985, p. 5).

Barrows designed a series of problems that went beyond conventional case studies. He didn't give students all the information but required them to research a situation, develop appropriate questions, and produce their own plan to solve the problem. This cultivated students' "clinical reasoning process" as well as their understanding of the tools at their disposal. He found that PBL also developed students' abilities to extend and improve their knowledge to keep up in the ever-expanding field of medicine and to learn how to provide care for new illnesses they encountered. Students who were taught through PBL became "self-directed learners" with the desire to know and learn, the ability to formulate their needs as learners, and the ability to select and use the best available resources to satisfy these needs. Barrows and Tamblyn defined this new method, problem-based learning, as "the learning that results from the process of working toward the understanding or resolution of a problem" (Barrows and Tamblyn 1980, p. 18). They summarized the process as follows:

1. The problem is encountered first in the learning sequence, before any preparation or study has occurred.

2. The problem situation is presented to the student in the same way it would present in reality.

3. The student works with the problem in a manner that permits his ability to reason and apply knowledge to be challenged and evaluated, appropriate to his level of learning.

4. Needed areas of learning are identified in the process of work with the problem and used as a guide to individualized study.

5. The skills and knowledge acquired by this study are applied back to the problem, to evaluate the effectiveness of learning and to reinforce learning.

6. The learning that has occurred in work with the problem and in individualized study is summarized and integrated into the student's existing knowledge and skills (Barrows and Tamblyn 1980, pp. 191–192).

Problem-Based Learning and the School Improvement Movement

Although the PBL method outlined in the preceding section originally was designed for medical schools, it has been adopted by a growing number of K–12 schools working to raise student achievement. Students educated for the world of the 21st century must develop habits of thinking, researching, and problem solving to succeed in a rapidly changing world. Yet, too many children in traditional education are not developing these increasingly vital abilities.

Thinking and problem-solving skills are not explicitly measured on a national basis. But studies show that while students are making progress in learning basic skills, only a small percentage perform at desired grade levels and master higher-order thinking.

For example, on the National Assessment of Educational Progress (NAEP) reading test, 57 percent of 17-year-olds scored below the level necessary to "find, understand, summarize, and explain relatively complicated literary and informational material" (National Center for Education Statistics 1996, p. 114). Only 10 percent of students scored in the top two levels (proficient and advanced) on the NAEP history test. And while more than half of 17-year-olds (59 percent) could answer "moderately complex procedures and reasoning," only 7 in 100 showed a mastery of "multi-step problem solving and algebra" (National Center for Education Statistics 1996, p. 122). In science, less than half (47 percent) could "analyze scientific procedures and data," with only 10 percent able to "integrate specialized scientific information" (National Center for Education Statistics 1996, p. 126). Clearly, while students are taught the basics, they are unable to proceed to understanding and using advanced knowledge.

Problem-based learning fits right into the movement for higher standards and greater achievement. PBL asks students to demonstrate an understanding of the material, not just to parrot back information with a few word changes. Research and teachers' experience have demonstrated that active instructional techniques like PBL can motivate bored students and raise their understanding and achievement. These student-centered strategies build critical thinking and reasoning skills, further students' creativity and independence, and help students earn a sense of ownership over their own work.

In classrooms where educators employ active learning strategies, students talk to each other, not through the teacher, and they initiate and manage many of their own activities. In these classes, the teacher serves as a guide to learning, providing room for students to increase their independence and build their own creativity. The teachers rely less on textbooks, using them as only one of a number of valid information sources that include everything from the Internet to community members. Similarly, schools using active learning become more flexible, allowing teachers greater freedom to direct their students and structure their own courses. They recognize that helping students master information needed to solve a problem and building their analytical reasoning skills are at least as important as memorizing a predetermined answer.

Present State of Problem-Based Learning

Since Barrows first used PBL at McMaster University in the mid-1960s, PBL "has caused a small revolution in the medical community" (Albanese

and Mitchell 1993), and it was cited by a *U.S. News and World Report* issue
reviewing medical schools:

> Since the late 1970s, New Mexico has been a pioneer in re-
> forming medical education and training. . . . It was the first
> U.S. medical school to embrace a curriculum built around a
> case study method—the problem-based approach adopted six
> years later by Harvard (Sarnoff 1996, pp. 92–94).

PBL is presently used in more than 60 medical schools worldwide
and also in schools of dentistry, pharmacy, optometry, and nursing. It is
also used in high schools, middle schools, and elementary schools in
cities, suburban counties, and rural communities. Teachers have been
trained at the Problem-Based Learning Institute in Springfield, Illinois; the
Center for Problem-Based Learning at the Illinois Mathematics and Science Academy in Chicago; and the Center for the Study of Problem-Based
Learning at Ventures In Education in New York City.

PBL offers K–12 teachers a structured method to help their students
build thinking and problem-solving skills while students master important subject knowledge. It empowers students with greater freedom while
providing a process that teachers can use to guide and lead students.
Most of all, PBL transfers the active role in the classroom to students
through problems that connect to their lives and procedures that require
them to find needed information, think through a situation, solve the
problem, and develop a final presentation.

At this point, you may wish to look at one of the "practical" chapters
(Chapters 7 to 11) before proceeding. Reading through some actual PBL
problems may help you understand the background information in Chapters 2 to 6.

2 Why Use Problem-Based Learning in Classrooms?

Just as medical students need to develop their capability to discover and use information, today's K–12 students need to build their own problem-solving skills and thinking abilities while learning the content necessary to apply those skills. The curriculum that best prepares students to be productive workers and citizens for the next century will not cram them with today's facts and theories—which soon may be outdated—but will show them how to learn on their own and how to use the information they acquire. Modifying Barrows's goals for medical students, we could state that K–12 students need

- to learn a body of essential knowledge (core information),
- the ability to use knowledge effectively with problem situations in and out of school (understanding), and
- the ability to extend or improve that knowledge and to develop strategies for dealing with future problems (active use of knowledge).

Problem-based learning (PBL) works well with *all* students, making its strategies ideal for heterogeneous classrooms where students with mixed abilities can pool their talents collaboratively to invent a solution. These techniques also lend themselves to an interdisciplinary orientation since answering a problem frequently requires information from several academic areas. By allowing children to direct their own activities and by giving them greater responsibilities, teachers show them how to challenge themselves and learn on their own. Teachers who use active learning say they have seen their students learn more material, understand more ideas, and enjoy school more.

Problem-Based Learning and Real Life

Students make a greater attempt to understand and remember when they see connections between the material they study and their own lives. Students constantly ask why they need to study a subject or what use the information will be to them. PBL answers these questions by placing learning in the context of real life. Students acquire new knowledge or skills to solve a problem or complete a task that is highly relevant to their lives. *Problem-based learning deals with problems that are as close to real-life situations as possible.*

Consider an advanced English as a Second Language class where the teacher uses PBL. The high school students, who are from at least 10 different countries and speak as many languages, summarized items that they read in newspapers. The last person to share an item was the teacher, who summarized a story about an increase in the number of clothing factories that pay less than minimum wage and whose employees work in substandard conditions.

After reading the item themselves, students hold a very spirited discussion, since many of them have friends or relatives working in such places. Having deliberately chosen the item to generate this interest, the teacher says, "Since many of you know people who work in these factories or under similar conditions, why don't we see if there is anything we can do about it?" She presents them with the following problem statement:

> It has come to the attention of several community leaders that the working conditions of immigrants in many communities are substandard. You are a member of a community group that has been asked to investigate these working conditions. You are collaborating with several labor unions who wish to organize the workers. You will present a report containing recommendations to the State Labor Commission. In that report you will push for enforcement of current laws—and enactment of new laws—to protect the workers.

This task instantly captures students' attention because it is current, real, and relevant to their lives or the lives of people they know well. It provides a purpose to their work in learning how to read and write. Now they are not just reading stories and writing papers because the teacher has assigned them; they are reading and writing to accomplish the task and help improve the lives of others.

Problem-Based Learning and Active Engagement

In many classrooms, learning is a passive activity. Students take notes during a teacher's lecture and repeat the same information back on tests. When students read a chapter assigned by the teacher and respond to questions about it, the answers are found in the chapter and are already known by the teacher. Even in math and science classes, teachers rarely allow students to discover principles for themselves but instead present the mathematical techniques and scientific laws and then make assignments where students simply practice what they already have been taught.

By contrast, problem-based learning promotes students' active engagement with learning. Solving a PBL problem demands student participation. The teacher helps and advises but does not direct. Learning becomes the act of discovery as students examine the problem, research its background, analyze possible solutions, develop a proposal, and produce a final result. Not only is this active learning more interesting and engaging for students, it also develops a greater understanding of the material since students find the information for themselves and then actively use the information and their skills to complete the project.

For example, in an elementary school housing grades K–8, a teacher presents this problem to a class of 7th grade students:

> A number of children and their parents have complained about the food that is served in the school cafeteria. Their complaints range from the nutritional value of the food to the fact that the food does not reflect the cultures from which the children come. Your class has been asked by the principal to look into these complaints and to prepare a set of recommendations regarding the foods served in the school cafeteria.

This project requires students to become energetic learners. No one will give them the information, nor will all the answers be found consecutively in the same book. Solving this problem requires that students discover the complaints, investigate the charges, develop the best way of resolving the situation, and then communicate their proposal to others. By doing this they learn how to find information for themselves, how to solve problems, and how to make a convincing presentation of their solution. These are vital skills for both college and careers.

Problem-Based Learning and Interdisciplinary Learning

Students who are used to switching subjects throughout the day act surprised when their science teacher corrects spelling on lab reports or their English teacher refers to historical events that shaped a writer's work. They have been taught to see each subject as totally isolated from any others. However, in the world outside school, work rarely fits the narrow boundaries of a single academic discipline. A doctor needs skills in biology, chemistry, mathematics, psychology, and English. A newspaper reporter needs a knowledge of English and history as well as science and statistics.

This holds true for PBL projects that mirror real-world conditions. *Problem-based learning promotes an interdisciplinary approach.* Because PBL requires students to read and write, research and analyze, and think and calculate, the problems frequently cut across disciplines and lend themselves to interdisciplinary courses. This shows students the connections between and among the subjects, helps them make greater sense of their schooling as a unified whole, and helps them use their knowledge of one field to increase their understanding of another.

For example, an art teacher, a mathematics teacher, and a language arts teacher might work together to develop the following problem that students in each class could work together to solve:

> A new school is to be built for our neighborhood at a cost of $8 million. By law, 1.5 percent of this cost is to be devoted to the installation of art in the school. You are members of a committee that must do two things. The first is to set up rules for the artists who wish to submit proposals, and the second is to determine how the school will select the art.

The very nature of this task requires students to be involved in elements from each discipline:

- language arts activities (reading, writing, speaking, and defining the school's identity);
- art activities (developing criteria for selection and studying different styles of art); and
- mathematics (calculating 1.5 percent of the cost and deciding the square footage allocated).

Problem-Based Learning and Student Choice

With the continuing explosion of knowledge and the rapid pace of technological change, schools can no longer present students with all the information they need for their entire lives. Increasingly, the most important skill schools can teach students is how to learn on their own. Working on PBL problems develops this skill to a greater degree than traditional teaching because once a problem is assigned, everything else is student driven.

Problem-based learning requires students to make choices about how and what they will learn. PBL students learn by working in teams and achieve success not through a teacher telling them they are right but through testing their solution and developing a presentation. For example, in a 4th grade class, the teacher presents the children with the following problem:

> The state legislature is considering changes to the New York State Constitution. An advocacy group is proposing a Bill of Rights for Children and wishes you and your classmates to make some suggestions for items to be included in the bill. You will propose items to the Bill of Rights and include reasons why these rights are needed.

With PBL, the teacher won't assign areas for students to research or create a checklist of sources to examine. Instead, the PBL process provides a structure for students to generate their own ideas and issues. First they brainstorm ideas that could be possible solutions or ideas that could lead to solutions once more information is known. Then they list facts based on what they know from the problem or their prior knowledge.

Next they consider learning issues that they believe should be researched before building a solution. Once these lists are generated, each student or group of students selects one or more of these learning issues and develops an action plan for how they will conduct their research. In this way, each student or group of students determines what to investigate and how to go about investigating it. Similarly, they develop the final product or presentation on their own, based on their ideas and the information they have discovered. While students may need additional guidance the first few times they tackle PBL, with practice they will understand the process and take greater responsibility for their own learning.

Problem-Based Learning and Collaborative Learning

Problem-based learning promotes collaborative learning. Students using PBL build teamwork skills as they learn from each other and work together to solve the problem. For this reason, PBL is ideal for classes with a range of academic abilities. Students in each group can work on different aspects of the problem. Similarly, students from diverse backgrounds will see different aspects of the problem and have varying ideas that could lead to solutions. Students develop leadership abilities through taking charge of their own team or through helping others with their research. For example, students in an 8th grade social studies class might be assigned the following problem:

> There has been a great deal of discussion about violence in the schools. Some schools have adopted dress codes as part of the solution and your school, although peaceful, is now considering a dress code as a preventive measure. You and your classmates have been asked to write a report on the effect dress codes have on the behavior of students.

Students in several groups could work together to research different learning issues, ranging from the legal rights of students to the effectiveness of dress codes in other schools. They then would share the information with the whole class, so each group depends on the others to find part of the information to solve the puzzle.

Problem-Based Learning and the Quality of Education

Problem-based learning helps raise the quality of education. With PBL strategies, teachers make the shift to higher standards and greater performance. The technique requires students to put forth more thought and effort than assignments requiring rote memorization. A well-written problem forces students to learn from a variety of different sources and to make decisions based on their research. This process enables students to meet standards calling for the development of advanced cognitive skills, research skills, and problem-solving skills.

As teachers use PBL, they develop new roles for themselves in the classroom that deepen their own understanding of teaching and learning. They move from the front of the classroom to the side, allowing students to take center stage. They allow students to interact more with each other instead of directing everything to the teacher. Instead of being the chief performer, the teacher is the conductor, guiding students through the learning process.

Furthermore, PBL helps connect students with the community and the larger world outside the classroom. Its emphasis on real-world problems takes students beyond textbooks and leads them to community resources. The product of a PBL exercise, such as a community recycling plan or a proposed playground layout, can be presented by students to the appropriate community body. Through solving PBL problems, students can participate in the civic life of their community and become better equipped to succeed in the adult world.

Ultimately, the true academic goal of PBL is not to develop a final answer to the problem. There is no single right answer that students will find and instantly agree is the "correct" solution. Instead, the actual learning takes place through the process of solving the problem—thinking through the steps, researching the issues, and developing the project.

3 The Teacher's Role in Problem-Based Learning

When observers who are unfamiliar with problem-based learning (PBL) peek into a PBL classroom, they probably find it very different from what they think of as "school." They don't see students seated in rows; instead, they see classmates working together in small groups or moving from one table of reference materials to another. They may expect absolute quiet as students listen to the teacher, but they hear the buzz of activity as groups hunt down needed information, determine how that knowledge will help them solve the problem, and then check to see if that information points the way to other needed information.

Observers won't instantly spot a teacher at the blackboard or lecturing in the front of the room; rather, they'll find the teacher at a student's desk commenting on the child's writing, in the corner making notes on class activity, or just about anyplace else in the room *except* the front. Seeing this, observers mistakenly may think that PBL requires very little of the teacher, who just seems to watch students work on their own. This is hardly the case. When one considers the time required to develop a problem, oversee and assist students throughout the project, encourage students to be more independent, and assess and evaluate the success of the problem as well as students' performance, it is clear that the teacher's role is vital for the effectiveness of this learning experience. In fact, many teachers think the PBL process requires more work than traditional lecturing, although it also offers greater rewards in exchange.

If problem-based learning is to develop student skills that result in greater retention and understanding, the teacher must play a different role than with traditional lessons. Though PBL teachers still decide what content knowledge, skills, and attitudes a problem should help students develop, they are no longer the center of attention as students learn.

Teachers guide students through the process of answering PBL questions, but they provide no answers themselves. They play their key role behind the scenes, designing the problem, subtly guiding students through it, and evaluating their performance. This backstage role is crucial in clearing the way for students to assume the "active" role in the project. In fact, students' success at solving the problem without constant direction is an indication of the teacher's success at using PBL.

Teachers have a different role in each stage of problem-based learning. First, the teacher develops the problem and fits it into the curriculum. Next, the teacher guides students through the problem. In the final stage, as students solve the problem, the teacher evaluates their performance.

The PBL Teacher as Curriculum Designer

The teacher's role as the creator of problems begins even before students arrive at the start of the school year. The teacher must decide if PBL should be the major teaching technique used throughout the entire course or if PBL should be used only at specific junctures.

For example, if a teacher decides to teach her entire biology course through PBL, she would first become thoroughly acquainted with the subject and any mandated content, reviewing materials with an eye for questions, information, and issues that she could make into good problems. She also would look at state and national standards both for issues that could be developed into problems and to ensure her course will teach the expected skills and attitudes. Then, before school starts, she would determine how best to organize her course's content and how the necessary material could be taught through PBL strategies.

Alternatively, a teacher might decide that it would be more appropriate to use PBL activities at specific points in the course. In this case the teacher would review the curriculum to find the best places for PBL activities. Again, the teacher would have to be familiar with content, skills, and attitudes required at local, state, and national levels.

Once the teacher has determined the content to be covered and the skills to be developed, the next step is to write a preliminary problem statement. The teacher should develop this problem (or choose one already written) from knowledge of individual student needs, values, interests, experiences, feelings, culture, and backgrounds. While the problem should be situated in the curriculum and teach useful knowledge and skills, at the same time it should link with students' experiences.

When PBL problems touch students' experiences and interests, students will be more actively involved and work harder at solving them. Problems may be generated in two ways. One way is a teacher or a group of teachers preparing them before the start of the school year. These problems address specific content and skills. An example of this type is described in Chapter 7 ("Oh, My Aching Stomach!"). The second way is when problems arise in the moment—students indicate an interest, and the teacher seizes the opportunity to teach through something that connects to their lives. An example is described in Chapter 11 ("Why Can't We Play?").

The PBL Teacher as Guide

In the second stage of problem-based learning, when the class works on the problem, the teacher assumes the role of guide, or facilitator. The teacher sets the climate, helps students connect to the problem, sets up a work structure, visits the problem with students, revisits the problem, facilitates the production of a product or a performance, and encourages self-evaluation.

Here, too, much of the work takes place backstage. The instructor must check on the resources available for research and alert school personnel if they will be contacted by students. If part of students' work will be a presentation before the city council, school board, or another group, the teacher will need to gauge these groups' receptiveness at being approached by students.

Teachers using PBL face the difficult task of guiding without leading and assisting without directing. Such work involves guiding students through the process of developing possible solutions, determining what they know and what they must find out, and deciding how they could answer their own questions. As students research and problem solve, teachers offer suggestions when students seem stuck and propose alternatives when their research or solutions do not appear to be adequate.

The PBL Teacher as Evaluator

Throughout the entire problem-based learning process, the teacher plays the role of evaluator. As an evaluator, the teacher monitors the effectiveness of the problem, the quality of students' work, and the teacher's own success in developing and facilitating the problem.

Effectiveness of the Problem

The teacher must determine the problem's success at developing students' knowledge and skills. A problem that is too easy or too difficult will not further students' growth. If this happens, the teacher may be able to modify the problem either by providing more information to the students or by altering the requirements for the presentation or project. At the end of the unit, the teacher may want to rewrite the problem for next year while the experience is still fresh.

Student Performance

Students should be evaluated not just for a grade but also to help them improve. In monitoring the class, the teacher should look for students having difficulty with the assignment and give them special help and suggestions. If large numbers of students have problems with part of the assignment, the teacher may find it necessary to make revisions to the problem or to classroom procedures.

Teacher Performance

Teachers must monitor their success to see if they are providing the right level of support and guidance for students. Remembering that part of the purpose of the lesson is to give students a greater sense of independence, the teacher should refrain from telling students information or what to do. At the end of the unit, teachers may want to write down a list of suggestions for how they could be more effective in future PBL work.

4 Developing a Problem

A large part of the art of instruction lies in making the difficulty of new problems large enough to challenge thought, and small enough so that, in addition to the confusion naturally attending the novel elements, there shall be luminous familiar spots from which helpful suggestions may spring.

—Dewey 1916, 1944, p. 157

Using problem-based learning (PBL) frees a teacher from the limitations of the textbook and the school's instructional materials. For a teacher using PBL, any incident or event, whether inside or outside the school, can spark a PBL problem that is linked to students' lives. For example, a teacher in a school with racial tensions could craft a problem on ways to promote greater understanding among different groups. During elections, teachers could create a PBL problem through which students develop a children's platform to send to candidates. Any issue or problem in which students have a personal interest or connection can become an effective PBL unit.

There is no limit to the variety of purposes behind PBL problems. Teachers can develop problems to address students' mastery of curriculum, to improve the community, or to solve interpersonal problems in the classroom. A problem can seek to change an unacceptable school or neighborhood situation or to celebrate a neighborhood achievement. Problems can be designed for part of a particular course, or they may be spread out throughout the curriculum. They can be specific to a single content area or interdisciplinary in nature; they can be designed by one teacher working alone or collaboratively for team teaching.

Whether selected from existing PBL materials or designed from scratch, problems should be developmentally appropriate, grounded in student experience, and curriculum based. Problems should accommodate a variety of teaching and learning strategies and styles, and they should promote the acquisition of knowledge as well as the development of skills. In addition, the problem should be ill-structured so that as students perform additional research, they discover the problem's complexity and understand that it may have a number of solutions.

Regardless of the purpose for which a problem has been selected and designed, a teacher generally follows the process of selecting content and skills, determining availability of resources, writing a problem statement, choosing a motivation activity, developing a focus question, and determining an evaluation strategy. Figure 4.1 contains a checklist for developing an ill-structured problem.

FIGURE 4.1

Checklist for Developing a Problem

Have I	Yes	No
Selected appropriate content?		
Determined availability of resources?		
Written a problem statement that • is developmentally appropriate? • is grounded in student experience?		
• is curriculum based?		
• allows for a variety of teaching and learning strategies and styles?		
• is ill-structured?		
Chosen a motivation activity?		
Developed a focus question?		
Determined evaluation strategies?		

Selecting Content and Skills

To select content objectives, a teacher would refer to curriculums developed by the district and the state. For example, a New York City teacher of 8th grade social studies would first go to New York City's *Curriculum Framework: Knowledge, Skills and Abilities Grades PreK–12* to find out what is required of that subject and grade:

> The Grade 8 program traces the human experience in the United States from 1816 to the present. It ties major political, economic, and social trends in United States history to parallel trends and time frames in New York State history (Board of Education of the City of New York 1995, p. 180).

The frameworks also have lists of what students would be expected to know and do by the end of the course. For example, consider these two points in the New York City framework:

- Demonstrate an awareness of the social, economic, and political changes in New York State and United States history, brought about by industrialization.

- Demonstrate an ability to access, analyze, evaluate, and present, orally or in writing, data related to New York State and United States history, brought about by industrialization (Board of Education of the City of New York 1995, p. 180).

Based on these frameworks and the current employment situation in New York City, the teacher could create a problem in which students act as a consulting firm hired by a corporation to produce alternatives to closing their old factory. Or the teacher could develop a problem on improving conditions in modern sweatshops.

In addition, teachers may consult standards and curriculums developed by national subject-specialty groups, such as the National Council of Teachers of Mathematics or the National Council on the Social Studies, for information and skills that could be included in PBL problems.

Once the teacher has determined the content of the PBL problem, the next stage is to determine what the students should be able to do by the time the problem is solved. The teacher also needs to decide how the problem could help students acquire those skills. For example, if the teacher believes that students need to improve their interpersonal skills, the problem could require them to interview other students and produce a group project. If the teacher believes students need to practice writing business letters, the problem could require writing to a manufacturer of a shoddy product. If the teacher wants students to read and discuss a specific author's canon of work, comparing and contrasting materials, the problem could ask them to develop a museum exhibition on the writer. The skills the problem should help students develop can come out of the teacher's own experience with the class, the curriculum, or the district's frameworks.

Determining Availability of Resources

A teacher does not want students to struggle with a project for lack of information. Before writing or choosing a problem, the teacher must ensure that students will be able to find the information necessary to solve it.

Generating lists of resources available in the classroom, school, and larger community could help students when they become stuck. The teacher also can check the resources available in the library or the school's procedures for using the Internet. Other staff members and community residents can be useful sources of information if they are available and accessible to students. Depending on building rules, students may be able to use the school's duplicating facilities, telephones, and fax machines. The district curriculum office or other district offices also may be of assistance.

Writing a Problem Statement

When the teacher has determined content and skills objectives and collected the necessary resources, the next step is to write the problem statement. A problem statement should

- be developmentally appropriate,
- be grounded in student experience,
- be curriculum based,
- accommodate a variety of teaching and learning strategies and styles, and
- be ill-structured.

Developmentally Appropriate

Problem selection or design should take into account the intellectual development and social-emotional needs of students. For example, the question of prejudice and tension between groups is appropriate for middle and high school students:

> The principal of the school is concerned about the tensions that seem to exist between individuals and among different groups in the school. He wants to learn what can be done to lessen the tensions and foster more harmony among students. He has asked this class to prepare a presentation for him, his cabinet, and the school's student government.

Grounded in Student Experience

To build, as Dewey put it, "luminous familiar spots" into "problems large enough to challenge thought," these problems should be grounded in the experiences of students (Dewey 1916, 1944, p. 157). These experiences may be from students' homes or cultures or their peer groups. They may come indirectly from television, radio, or the movies, or they may be the result of school experiences. The closer the problem is to students' daily lives and something they care about, the harder they will work. For example, students' actual complaints about not being able to play on the school's basketball court led a teacher to draft the following problem:

> Several 5th and 6th graders have complained that the bigger children on the playground will not allow others to use the basketball area. You have been asked by the head teachers of the upper grades to look into the matter and come up with a series of recommendations that will allow any student who wishes to use the basketball court.

Curriculum Based

Problems should be vehicles by which students obtain knowledge from a variety of disciplines. Problems should promote the acquisition of appropriate skills and content knowledge found in the district's frameworks or the teacher's curriculum. Good problems creatively combine students' lives and what they see and do every day with topics from the

course syllabus. Problems could include material not normally studied if it helps students build important skills or leads them to important information. Problems may also explore links between subjects. For example, an art and English class might combine for a problem on public art:

> The subway station is going to be improved at a cost of $5 million. By law, 2 percent of this money is to be devoted to public art in the station. You are members of a committee that has two tasks. The first is to set up the rules and regulations for artists who wish to submit entries. The second is to determine the criteria or guidelines for selecting the winning designs.

Variety of Teaching and Learning Strategies and Styles

Teachers and students have different ways of teaching and learning. A problem should not be so rigid that it has only one right solution, one way of reaching a solution, or one way of instructing students. Problems should be designed to allow success for teachers with different teaching styles as well as for the variety of student learning styles in the classroom. The problem should promote a range of activities that allow students of different levels to contribute to the solution. For example, the following problem might be worked on by students individually or in groups, researching library materials, contacting publishers, or interviewing adults about books they use:

> The Caribbean, a region of islands populated by English-, French-, and Spanish-speaking inhabitants, is the former home of many of our students or their parents. Our school library does not contain materials that adequately reflect the culture of this region, and you have been asked to submit a plan for remedying this situation.

Ill-Structured

Unlike a thinking exercise that includes all necessary information or a traditional project that requires students to use information they already know, PBL problems should be designed so that students must perform research to gather the information needed for possible solutions. It should require students to think through information they already know and to find additional information, interpreting preexisting knowledge in light of new data they discover. In addition, the problem should lead students to discover that there may be a number of solutions.

For example, students in a class with large numbers of immigrants would find the following problem immediately relevant, and they already would know a great deal about immigration. However, solving the problem would require them to find specific figures about jobs, taxes, and the economic impact of immigrants:

> The newspapers have recently reported that many people are concerned about the number of immigrants arriving in the United States and how they are taking away jobs, being supported by taxpayers, and using up scarce resources. They are saying that we should no longer allow immigrants to come to the United States. You and your classmates have been asked by your state representative to look into these claims and to make some suggestions as to how he could deal with this issue.

Choosing a Motivation Activity

Once the teacher has written or chosen the problem, she should think of ways to show its connection to students' lives. Generally, the teacher deliberately includes relevance to students as one of the criteria for selecting or designing a problem. Still, the teacher should think of ways to introduce the subject and make the links explicit.

The greater students' involvement in an issue, the greater their investment in its solution and the harder they will work. For example, in the case of the social studies teacher using the preceding problem on immigration, she knows that many of her students come from immigrant families or have immigrant friends from such families, so this issue will touch them personally. The teacher can help build the issue in their minds by starting the class with articles calling for a reduction of benefits to immigrants or demanding a strong crackdown on illegal immigrants. The teacher can ask students if they know people who were born in other countries, and they can mark those countries on the map. This would lead into a discussion about immigration that then will make the students more excited about solving the problem.

Developing a Focus Question

Once the teacher has written the problem statement, she should develop a question that will help students focus on their task after they become interested in the problem. In the immigration problem, the teacher might ask, "Now that we've talked about immigration and know what problem we have to solve, let's focus on 'How is immigration good or bad for the country?' or 'How do immigrants use resources?'"

Determining an Evaluation Strategy

Evaluation strategies with problem-based learning are as varied as those used in any classroom. Mastery of content could be assessed using a pre-post test, or it could be assessed using a debate format where the teacher has a checklist of items to be rated on a five-point scale. For each problem, the teacher should integrate a product or performance that is used to evaluate mastery of content, skills, and the process of problem solving itself. Chapters 5 and 6 provide additional information on evaluation.

When students are motivated and understand the importance of an issue to their own lives, the teacher can introduce a carefully crafted problem that gains their full attention. Students who see the relevance of their work to their own lives are more likely to be active workers rather than passive observers, enthusiastic learners rather than reluctant listeners. Once a problem is developed and students are connected to it, the teacher can follow the PBL process as outlined in the remainder of this book.

5 The Problem-Based Learning Process

The freedom created by problem-based learning (PBL) makes it necessary for students to follow a carefully planned process if they are to experience success. This may sound contradictory, but the PBL process steers students through the complex tasks of brainstorming ideas, identifying useful knowledge, asking appropriate research questions, and crafting a strategy for finding answers. A carefully planned process helps students avoid blind alleys and prevents them from jumping to the next step without first building a stable platform.

The process used throughout this book has been implemented successfully in high schools, middle schools, and medical schools throughout the United States, and it has been described in a number of sources (Barrows and Tamblyn 1980, Barrows 1985, Problem-Based Learning Institute 1994). We organize the problem-based learning process into the following steps: connecting with the problem, setting up the structure, visiting the problem, revisiting the problem, producing a product or performance, and evaluating performance and the problem.

With PBL, students who normally take notes on the teacher's comments and answer the teacher's questions now find themselves asking the questions and answering others posed by their peers. Because of the enormity of this change, the teacher must create a climate in which students feel comfortable making suggestions and expressing their thoughts. If students feel that speaking out requires taking a risk, or that other students may make fun of their answers, they will not participate and the project will not work.

The success of a PBL lesson depends in large part on the teacher's success at setting up a series of guidelines to encourage students of all abilities to become involved. These guidelines create a risk-free environment in which every student's contribution is respected and valued. In addition, the teacher must make all students feel that they can contribute by either sharing new information or adding to information given by others. This is especially important in brainstorming but also when researching or working in groups. Above all, students must understand that they all need to participate for the class to succeed.

When describing this process to students, the teacher should explain that they must take the lead role in the project. The teacher might say something like, "Class, as we solve this problem we will be working a little differently from the way we've worked in the past. You will be doing most of the work of solving the problem and providing your own direction. I will be available to help you clarify your thoughts and suggest courses of action, but I will not give you answers or tell you when you are right or wrong. I'll be here as a resource for you, but in this project you will learn by discovering answers for yourself."

Connecting with the Problem

For the PBL unit to be effective, students should feel that the problem is important and worth their time and attention. The teacher selects or designs problems that are connected to things students care about in their daily lives: personal experiences; experiences of family or friends; or the television, film, or music that students enjoy.

This connection can be made through a preliminary reading or discussion, which introduces the topic in a concrete fashion. For example, one teacher wanted to introduce her advanced English as a Second Language (ESL) class to a PBL problem on whether English should be made the official language of the United States. She showed a clip from a television program in which "English only" was the topic. She then introduced the topic and led students in a brief discussion, inviting them to share their personal connections to this issue: "How many of you have heard that many people in the United States believe that we should have a law that says English should be our official language?"

When several students raised their hands to indicate they had heard of this, the teacher asked, "And what do you think about this?"

One student answered, "I think it's a good idea." Several others nodded in agreement, but some shook their heads no.

The teacher asked, "What about those of you who don't agree?"

Another student answered, "Well, if we can only speak English, what will my grandmother do?"

The teacher responded, "Do you think 'English only' means you can't speak your own language in your own home?"

The student replied, "Well, I heard about a mother out West who got into trouble because she spoke Spanish to her son at home."

Another student added, "But where I live, everybody speaks Spanish. I only hear English at school."

The teacher allowed this discussion to continue, knowing full well that her students would raise many issues. Instead of correcting misinformation, she allowed students to say what they believed, knowing it would be clarified by the end of the process.

When she decided that all of her students who wanted to speak had the chance to do so, she said, "Well, our project is to look into this situation and determine whether or not a law on this subject would be a good idea." She then presented students with the following problem statement:

> There are a number of people who believe that English should be the official language of the United States, and they advocate that a law be passed to this effect. You and your classmates have been asked to prepare a report on this issue and present it to your state representative.

Setting Up the Structure

Once the teacher is sure that students have made a connection with the issue, the next step is to create the structure for working through the problem. This structure provides a framework on which students can build their project. It ensures that students' work has a proper foundation and that none of the essential elements is neglected. The structure is key to the whole PBL process, showing students how to think through the situation and reach an appropriate solution.

The teacher starts by reminding students that they will be the ones responsible for solving the problem. Then the teacher says that throughout the process they will be asked to note information on a large sheet of paper. She asks for volunteers to act as recorders: "I'd like to have two people who would be willing to come to the front of the room to act as recorders. Remember that when you are a recorder, you will have to listen very carefully so that you can record what people want written down."

The teacher emphasizes the need to record exactly what students want on the sheet. Accurate recording reminds students of what has been said and also sends the message that their statements are valued. Then the teacher points out, "We also need volunteers who will record at their desks. We need this just in case we have to check on the accuracy of what is recorded up front and so that each group has a copy of the chart."

Having more than one recorder provides alternate records in case one student leaves something out. Also, this provides a chance for more students to be actively involved in the early stages of the project.

At this point, the teacher begins to introduce the chart that's on the paper she posted. She tells students, "Let's look at what we are going to put up on the piece of paper. We are going to divide the paper into four columns. Those of you taking notes at your desk can do the same. We will label the first column 'Ideas.' In this column, the recorders will write down any ideas that you have about possible solutions to the problem. Remember that each of you has ideas that are very valuable, and you should share them with the class. Please do not comment on or object to other people's ideas. Right now we are trying to put as many ideas as we can in this column. Later we will decide what ideas we wish to develop." Figure 5.1 depicts this first part of the chart.

FIGURE 5.1

Column 1 Heading in the Chart for the PBL Process

Ideas			

Students then fill the ideas column with their possible solutions or ways to solve the problem. It is imperative for the teacher to attempt to get all students involved in the generation or discussion of items listed in this column.

It may seem counterintuitive to have students suggest solutions before beginning research. However, by listing their ideas, students will be able to see what research they need to do to determine which solution is the best. This is similar to a scientist developing a hypothesis before beginning to develop the experiment or an author writing an outline that is then filled in through research. The teacher should emphasize that students need not feel committed to the ideas in this column, and later in the process they can add additional ideas suggested by research.

Next the teacher points out, "The second column will be labeled 'Facts.' In this column we'll record facts that we know about this problem. You can find some facts in the problem or from the discussion we just had. If we know any facts from previous courses, books we've read, or movies or television we've seen, we can record these as well. If there is some disagreement over whether or not something is a fact, then we will have to do some research and find out more about it." The teacher now labels the second column as shown in Figure 5.2.

Students will fill the facts column with information embedded in the problem statement as well as information they already know. This will ensure that all students start the process with the same information and that students do not use research time finding information that others in the class already could tell them. This column serves as a resource pool or a bank of knowledge from which students will draw information to solve

FIGURE 5.2

Column 1 and 2 Headings in the Chart for the PBL Process

Ideas	Facts		

the problem. Also, being able to see all the facts at once may help students develop additional areas to examine.

During the discussion of items in this column, the teacher can show students how to distinguish between fact and opinion. If students are not positive that a suggestion is a fact, or if the teacher thinks there is room to question it, the suggestion can be moved to the third column and investigated during the research stage.

Next the teacher points to the third column: "Let's take those suggestions that we were not sure about and put them in the third column, 'Learning Issues.' In this column we will record the questions we still have. This will show us what we need to know to help us come up with a solution to the problem. We can have the recorders write questions we want answered, definitions we need, or just general topics we need to research." Figure 5.3 shows this third column.

The learning issues column encompasses items that need further elaboration, definition, or research. Some of these questions are developed by students, and others are items from the facts column that need to be checked. In addition, the teacher can help students suggest other areas for exploration by probing for depth of understanding. For example, she might ask, "Does everyone understand John's explanation of ratios? Do you think we might want to find out some more information about it? Yes? Well, let's put it up as a learning issue." Or, the teacher might ask, "Can you tell me more about this process of neutralizing? Do you think we should do some research on it? Or maybe we could do a lab experiment to find out about it. Should it go up as a learning issue?"

FIGURE 5.3

Column 1, 2, and 3 Headings in the Chart for the PBL Process

Ideas	Facts	Learning Issues	

These learning issues are a guide, serving as the basis for students' research and suggesting areas for further investigation. The learning issues column also is the list of questions from which students will choose the line of research they want to pursue. Without such planning, it would be too easy for students to lose themselves in the information jungle, unsure of exactly what they need to find.

Finally the teacher points out, "The last column is called 'Action Plan.' This is where we will record how we will perform our research. This can include people who know the answers we need, books on our topic, computer CD-ROMs, the Internet, or experts we can call." Figure 5.4 shows the now-complete skeleton of the organizing chart.

FIGURE 5.4

Column Headings in the Chart for the PBL Process

Ideas	Facts	Learning Issues	Action Plan

At this stage in the process, students develop a plan to find the information they need. They list the resources they can use to address the learning issues, and they propose strategies for how to proceed. The teacher guides them to generate a variety of sources that goes beyond textual materials and includes all available resources in the school.

The teacher may wish to use other headings for these columns to make them clearer for the children. Headings should be appropriate to students' age and understanding.

Visiting the Problem

Once the teacher has explained how they are going to proceed, she asks someone to reread the problem statement. She focuses on having students generate ideas for how to solve the problem, recognizing that they may want other columns filled in as well. Next, the focus turns to generating facts as well as a list of items that need further clarification.

These are recorded in the column labeled "Learning Issues." Periodically, the teacher asks students to summarize what has been recorded.

When the three columns are filled, the teacher says: "Let's go back to our ideas column and read through the list of possible solutions we have generated. What we need to do now is for each one of us to choose an idea that we think would be the best solution to the problem."

Each student or group of students chooses an idea to examine. Once committed, the students or groups are then asked to look at the learning issues and to select one or more of those questions to research. Students can choose questions that will support their proposed solution or questions that personally intrigue them. Since all information will be shared before the students work on the product or presentation, each group should look at different questions (or use different resources on the same questions to provide alternative viewpoints).

Now the teacher suggests, "Once you have selected an issue or issues to research, you need to share with us how you are going to go about researching it. What resources are you going to use? Computer, textbooks, experiments, interviews, experts? How will you use your time?"

Students then turn to the final column to see what sources would have the most information about their questions. Using the information in the last two columns, they prepare a plan of attack that will shape their research.

The teacher then tells the students how many periods they have to do their independent work and lets them begin. Throughout the research, the teacher moves from one student or group to another, suggesting areas to explore or additional sources that might help. But the teacher *does not* provide any actual answers. The teacher may stay with a group for 30 seconds or 10 minutes, depending on what is needed. It is during this period of independent research that the teacher is able to assess students' research skills. When students have completed their research, the teacher reconvenes the class.

Revisiting the Problem

After they complete their independent work, students reassemble as a class and revisit the problem. The teacher first has each student or group report on their work. At the same time the teacher assesses the resources students used, their use of time, and the overall effectiveness of their action plan.

At this point the teacher might suggest, "Now that you've done the research, I want you to look at your original idea. Do you still want to be committed to it? Do you think you proved it? Do you think you disproved it? What information do you have that supports this position?"

The teacher asks each individual or group to answer these questions. Students are given the chance to tell how the facts they found support or disprove the ideas in the first column. On a separate sheet of paper, and using different color markers to indicate new data, the recorders list the facts supporting and opposing each solution.

Now students may have additional questions based on research done by other groups, or they may notice new solutions. If so, the teacher might want to allow additional research time for students to examine these new questions or solutions. In this second round of research, groups may decide to examine a solution that is different from the one they researched the first time. If not, the class or groups can vote on which solution they want to pursue for their project.

For example, students working on advising their representative about establishing English as the official U.S. language could choose from a number of solutions:

- a Constitutional amendment,
- further investigation of the group's claims, or
- support for a "Declaration of Diversity."

Students would examine each of these suggestions in light of the facts reported by the class and those discovered in research. The class then would select the proposed solution that had the most information showing it would work, or that is true to their principles and beliefs—but may not succeed.

In this stage students learn how to weigh the evidence and to make comparisons between and among different ideas. They develop skills in analysis and decision making. Because students must defend their ideas with facts and persuade other students to support their proposed solution, this part of the PBL assignment further develops their communication skills and persuasive speaking abilities.

Producing a Product or Performance

Each problem concludes with a student product or performance. This can range from writing a letter to the editor to making a presentation before a community board. The product or performance is designed to enable the teacher to evaluate both content objectives and mastery of selected skills. It further strengthens students' understanding of the material by requiring them to use it to accomplish a task. For example, students may be able to recite a textbook definition of *ratio,* but using ratios to build a model of a playground to scale leads students to understand and remember the concept.

The product lends a sense of purpose to the entire PBL assignment. Students go through the process and research their questions to have material for their product. Also, the teacher can use the final product to measure student success at meeting learning outcomes.

The product or performance may take many forms, depending on the teacher's objectives. Generally, the product will either have different parts that can be built by individuals or groups, or different groups could produce different projects. For example, if a class decides to recommend that their representative oppose "English only" legislation, each group could write a letter exploring a different reason for this position. Alternatively, the whole class could prepare an Advisory Committee Report, with each group writing a different chapter.

Evaluating Performance and the Problem

At the end of the unit, the teacher encourages students to evaluate their own performance, their group's performance, and the quality of the problem itself. Initially this may present students with some difficulties, so the teacher may wish to provide them with a self-evaluation form, such as the one shown in Figure 5.5 (see p. 36). As students become adept at evaluating themselves, however, they may no longer need such a model.

The teacher can also use this evaluation when writing additional problems or to determine where students need additional guidance with their next PBL problem. This student self-evaluation is in addition to the teacher's evaluation, which is described in Chapter 6.

FIGURE 5.5

Student Self-Evaluation Form

Student: Class: Date:

Activity	Excellent	Good	Fair
I contributed ideas/facts.			
I came up with some learning issues.			
I used a variety of resources when doing my research.			
I helped think through the problem.			
I contributed new information.			
I helped my group in doing its work.			

The process outlined in this chapter is intended as a guide, not a straitjacket. It provides a launching point for students' explorations without limiting their range. It reduces the potential confusion while still leaving the creativity. Following the process requires students to think through each step before moving on to the next, and it prevents them from jumping too far ahead of themselves. It will give them a basis for gathering information and making decisions about which solution is best. It also helps teachers keep track of what students have already figured out and what they still need to learn.

6 Evaluating Problem-Based Learning in the Classroom

In most classrooms, evaluation takes the form of a test or paper showing what students have learned. The process of evaluation in a problem-based learning (PBL) classroom, however, is more encompassing in its methods, procedures, and goals. With problem-based learning, evaluation is integrated throughout the process as the teacher observes students' abilities during each step of solving the problem.

Although a final product or performance is an integral part of problem-based learning, Barrows notes:

> It should be understood by the students at the outset that this [final product] is a vehicle for the evaluation of [their] . . . learning with the problem and their communication and performance skills (Barrows 1994, p. 2).

In addition, teachers should evaluate the PBL problem itself and their own success in using it.

Student Evaluation

Assessment of student performance begins the first day a PBL problem is introduced and lasts until the final product is reviewed. The teacher keeps track of student achievement and understanding, modifying the lesson and instruction accordingly. The teacher pays close attention to students' abilities to think through each of the problem-solving steps, the level of their self-direction, and their ability to work together. In addition, the teacher monitors the mastery of content as well as students' development of selected skills.

For example, an 8th grade teacher in an inner-city school may start a unit on civic rights and duties by discussing recent articles on the President's support of curfews for teenagers. After a lively debate on the issue, he presents his students with the following problem statement:

> Many large cities are adopting curfews for people under 18 years of age. The Justice Department recently reported that curfews are in effect in 146 of the nation's 200 largest cities, with generally good results. Many people support curfews; however, many others do not. The city council has asked your class to help them decide on a new curfew law by researching the topic and making both oral and written presentations for both sides of the issue.

To meet his objectives for this unit, the teacher has carefully written this problem to require his students to produce both a product and performance. The product requirement—the oral and written presentations of both sides of the issue—allows him to assess improvements in students' abilities to

- organize and synthesize material,
- use appropriate research data,
- speak before a group, and
- create a reasoned paper or presentation.

The performance requirement—doing the necessary research for the paper and presentation—allows the teacher to determine students' progress in developing the abilities to

- use varied research tools, such as an atlas or a CD-ROM with census data;
- interview sources; and
- collect and organize information.

For both, the teacher can use a checklist to record observations.

In addition to collecting information on the student products and performances, the teacher also collects data on students engaged in the

PBL process to ensure that they are developing necessary problem-solving skills. Using the steps in the PBL process as a guide, the teacher formulates a series of questions that allow him to measure each student's engagement in the process and the engagement of the class as a whole. Figure 6.1 (see p. 40) contains a list of questions to help the teacher make this assessment.

Teachers may wish to use the forms in Figures 6.2 (see pp. 41–42) and 6.3 (see p. 43) to help organize their thoughts for student evaluation and for future work with a problem.

Teacher Evaluation

While reflecting on student performance, the teacher also should analyze his own skill with guiding students rather than directly instructing them. The teacher should ask questions such as those in Figure 6.4 (see p. 44).

Figures 6.5 (see p. 45) and 6.6 (see p. 46) contain forms teachers might want to use while evaluating their performance.

Problem Evaluation

While evaluating students and their own performance, teachers should also ask themselves questions to reexamine the effectiveness of the problem itself:

- Did the problem meet key curriculum goals?
- Did the problem build students' thinking and reasoning skills?
- Did the problem connect the outside world with the inside world?
- Did the problem emerge from the concerns of students and evoke their interests?
- Was the problem the right level for the students?
- Could students solve the problem with the resources available?
- Are changes necessary before this problem is used with this level of students again?

Figure 6.7 (see p. 47) contains a sample "Problem Evaluation Checklist."

(text continues on p. 42.)

FIGURE 6.1

Evaluating Student and Class Engagement in the PBL Process

Setting the Climate
What were students' responses to my less prominent role?
How did students react to the conditions I set?

Connecting with the Problem
Did students respond to the problem? How did they respond?
Did they share personal experiences?
Did they connect through television, film, radio, or the experiences of their peers?
Were they engaged in the topic?

Setting Up the Structure
Did students volunteer to act as recorder, either at the front of the room or in their seats?

Visiting the Problem
Did they generate ideas?
Did they use information from the problem as well as from previous courses?
Did they generate learning issues from ideas and facts?
Did they think of a variety of sources?

Revisiting the Problem
Did they connect their information to the problem?
Did they reevaluate the ideas or hypotheses they had generated?
Did they generate additional issues?

Producing a Product or Performance
Did all students participate?
Did they use the information in the product correctly?
Did they produce a high-quality product using their full effort?

Evaluating Performance and the Problem
How did the students evaluate themselves as members of a group and as individuals?

FIGURE 6.2

Example of a Student or Class Record for Evaluating Engagement in the PBL Process

Student/Class: 8-106   Problem: Curfew   Level: 8   Dates: 2/5–2/9

OBSERVATIONS

Setting the Climate: Since this was midyear, students were comfortable with each other. Two new students had not yet found a place in class.

Connecting with the Problem: Class was immediately interested in and very vocal about this particular issue. Many had heard about it on TV and some had read about it. Others had read interviews with teenagers done by a local paper.

Setting Up the Structure: Class divided into groups. They are accustomed to working this way.

Visiting the Problem
- **Generates ideas/hypotheses**
  Class able to generate a great many ideas both pro and con.
- **Recalls facts/information**
  Facts from problem listed but few others.
  Many students related personal experiences.
- **Formulates learning issues**
  Difficult to generate. Most wanted to look into anecdotal
    material.
- **Develops plan of action**
  Most say go to library, look at newspapers.

Revisiting the Problem
- **Evaluates resources**
  Difficult to assess in this area. No one used census data.
  Few looked up cities. No one seemed to use atlas. Did not
    distinguish between news articles and editorials.
- **Reexamines ideas/hypotheses**
  Most were able to do this.
- **Connects information to problem**
  Groups had some difficulty here. They were easily side-
    tracked.

(Figure continues on the following page.)

FIGURE 6.2

(Continued)

Producing a Product or Performance
- **Incorporates information into product**
  Most of the research was used in their presentations, but
  some assumptions were not supported by the evidence.
- **Participates in creating product**
  All students played important roles in writing the report and
  presentation.
- **Other**
  Students wanted to jump right to the writing immediately.
  They had difficulty understanding the planning stage.

Evaluating Performance and the Problem: Most felt they
did well. They had difficulty in assessing others in group.

Comments: Need to focus on following: validity of anecdotal
source material vs. data based; use of variety of resources;
evaluation of source material; and summarizing skills.

By the end of the PBL activity, the teacher has watched students
brainstorm possible solutions, review their knowledge, determine key
questions, develop research methodology to find facts, conduct research,
fit research to the problem to develop a solution, explain their reasoning
to the class, produce a final product, and present the product. Throughout each of these stages the teacher evaluates each student's performance,
both individually and as part of a group. In addition, teachers of PBL
assess their effectiveness as facilitators of the process and the success of
the problem at increasing what students know and can do. Although
these forms and questions are a useful guide, every teacher needs to
determine the specificity of evaluation required to assess class performance, to improve the next PBL activity, or to give students a grade.

FIGURE 6.3

Student or Class Record Showing Rating System

Student/Class: Problem: Level: Dates:

EVALUATION	RATING		
	1 (Excellent)	2 (Good)	3 (Fair)
Setting the Climate			
Connecting with the Problem			
Setting Up the Structure			
Visiting the Problem			
Generates ideas/hypotheses			
Recalls facts/information			
Formulates learning issues			
Develops plan of action			
Revisiting the Problem			
Evaluates resources			
Reexamines ideas/ hypotheses			
Connects information to problem			
Producing a Product or Performance			
Incorporates information into product			
Participates in creating product			
Other			
Evaluating Performance and the Problem			

Comments:

FIGURE 6.4

Self-Evaluating Teacher Performance in the PBL Process

Setting the Climate
Did I create a no-risk environment? What new risks were
they willing to take?
Did I model for my students?
Did I have the appropriate resources?

Connecting with the Problem
Did I make the problem interesting for students?
How many ways did students connect with the problem?
Did they connect through personal experience, media,
discussion, or readings?

Setting Up the Structure
Did I ensure that the students understood the problem
and the process?
Did I gradually withdraw from the process?
Did I allow the students to eventually direct the process?
Did I operate at a high enough level?
Did I ensure thinking would be paramount?

Visiting the Problem
Did I have students use their own resources?
Did I probe enough?
Did I encourage independence?
Did I facilitate higher-level thinking?
Did I encourage reflection?
Did I move the group along at an appropriate pace?
Did I ensure that each student would be successful?

Producing a Product or Performance
Did I ensure that all of my students contributed?
Did I ensure that their efforts were validated? Did I
provide guidance without taking control?

Evaluating Performance and the Problem
Did I create an atmosphere of trust in which students felt
comfortable evaluating themselves and each other
fairly and honestly?

FIGURE 6.5

Example of a Teacher Self-Evaluation Form for the PBL Process

Student/Class: 8-106   Problem: Curfew   Level: 8   Dates: 2/5–2/9

REFLECTIONS

Setting the Climate: Instructions and explanations enabled class to feel comfortable with their role as PBL learners.

Connecting with the Problem: Preliminary activity led to personal investment in solving the problem. Need to be less defensive on relevance to their lives.

Setting Up the Structure: Asking current students to explain the process to new students worked well because they had done PBL before.

Visiting the Problem: Making chart went well, but had some difficulty helping students generate learning issues. Need to explain difference between anecdotal and data-based information.

Revisiting the Problem: Students had some difficulty in evaluating resources and reexamining ideas in light of information gathered. Need lesson on how to evaluate resources.

Producing a Product or Performance: Need to stand back a little further and give students a greater sense of independence. Need to make myself available but encourage students to try their own ideas first.

Evaluating Performance and the Problem: Students still need some work on how to do self-evaluation as well as peer evaluation. Perhaps let students do anonymous evaluations. Difficulty was complicated by developmental issues.

Comments: All students were actively involved. This points out need for this kind of involvement in all curriculum areas. Need to rethink some problems in English and biology.

FIGURE 6.6

Example of a Teacher Self-Evaluation Rating Form

Student/Class: Problem: Level: Dates:

EVALUATION	1 (Excellent)	2 (Good)	3 (Fair)
Setting the Climate: Instructions and explanations enabled class to feel comfortable with their role as PBL learners.			
Connecting with the Problem: Preliminary activity led to personal investment in solving the problem. Need to be less defensive on relevance to their lives.			
Setting Up the Structure: Asking current students to explain the process to new students worked well because they had done PBL before.			
Visiting the Problem: Making chart went well, but had some difficulty helping students generate learning issues. Need to explain difference between anecdotal and data-based information.			
Revisiting the Problem: Students had some difficulty in evaluating resources and reexamining ideas in light of information gathered. Need lesson on how to evaluate resources.			
Producing a Product or Performance: Need to stand back a little further and give students a greater sense of independence. Need to make myself available but encourage students to try their own ideas first.			
Evaluating Performance and the Problem: Students still need some work on how to do self-evaluation as well as peer evaluation. Perhaps let students do anonymous evaluations. Difficulty was complicated by developmental issues.			

FIGURE 6.7

Problem Evaluation Checklist

Student: _____ Problem: _____ Date: _____

EVALUATION	RATING		
	1 (Excellent)	**2** (Good)	**3** (Fair)
Did the problem • meet key curriculum goals? • facilitate skills development? • build reasoning skills? • allow students to connect with it? • promote the use of a variety of resources?			
Can the problem be used at this level?			

7

11th–12th Grade Chemistry Problem: "Oh, My Aching Stomach!"

Scientists are problem-based learners. When confronted with a question to investigate, they begin by researching information, using it to develop a hypothesis, determine how to prove that hypothesis, and then develop the final product. Consequently, science classes naturally lend themselves to problem-based learning (PBL) activities.

Most science classes already use hands-on scientific experiments similar to PBL where students learn through performing actions and the process is more important than the final result. (However, while science lab work often has step-by-step instructions and a definite right answer, PBL is more open-ended with students determining both their course of action and the end result.) Science teachers can easily adapt experiment-oriented lesson plans to PBL, and they already are familiar with how to assist students working in groups.

Recognizing this similarity, teacher Carl Miller has redesigned his high school chemistry course using the problem-based learning format. He has found that many of his urban students tune him out when he stands in front of the board lecturing, but they actively participate when given an experiment to conduct or a problem to solve.

Mr. Miller incorporates a variety of resources in this course, and he has integrated a number of lab activities and a series of demonstrations into the problems. "Oh, My Aching Stomach!" is a two- to three-week unit on acids and bases. It is the 13th of 16 problems he has developed for his chemistry class.

Connecting with the Problem

Mr. Miller starts each lesson with a lead-in connecting the problem to experiences his students have had, have read about, or have seen on film or television. He knows that the more connections his students can make between their lives and the problem being studied, the more energy and involvement they will generate. He opens with, "How many of you have ever been in a situation where, after a big family meal, someone says 'That didn't agree with my stomach. I have heartburn.' Or have you heard someone say, 'I need something to settle my stomach!'?"

Almost everyone in the room has something to contribute. Mr. Miller allows comments to continue until all have participated. At that point he says, "I think we all have been in such situations, and the response has probably been the same: Go to the medicine chest to get something to settle your stomach. Our problem today relates to an upset stomach. What causes stomachs to misbehave in this fashion and what can be done to fix it?" At this point Mr. Miller presents the problem:

> Several of your relatives or other people you know have had problems with upset stomachs or indigestion and have gone to their doctors. Their doctors tell them that their upset stomach or indigestion is caused by too much stomach acid, and they prescribe over-the-counter antacids. Your relatives, however, are confused. They really don't understand acid and antacid and don't know which product to choose. You and your group are to help them understand what is happening in their stomachs and how to go about choosing the right product.

Since this situation has happened in most families—and students are familiar with the problem from television advertisements—Mr. Miller is sure that his students will have a high level of interest and involvement. Students will help their families and learn information that will be useful later in life.

Setting Up the Structure

Earlier in the year, Mr. Miller spelled out each step of the PBL process as they went along. At this point, his students are very familiar with PBL, but Mr. Miller still takes some time at the start of each problem to refresh their memories about the process. He asks students to explain the column arrangement in the organizing chart, the need for class and group recorders, and the need to listen carefully to what is being said. He also reiterates the point that when someone makes a contribution, he will assume that everyone agrees on the point if no one comments on it or if there is silence. Finally, he reminds them that although they will proceed through one column at a time, there will be times when a suggestion will be placed in a different column than the one with which they are working.

Visiting the Problem

At this point Mr. Miller asks a student to read the problem, and he invites all to suggest ideas, as shown in Figure 7.1 (see p. 51).

Next he asks students to list the facts they already know about indigestion, shown in Figure 7.2 (see p. 52). Mr. Miller knows some important facts were not stated, but he does not reveal them to the class because he knows they will be discovered when students begin their research and investigation.

Satisfied that the facts have been listed, Mr. Miller then goes on to the learning issues column, shown in Figure 7.3 (see p. 53).

After students have generated a list of what they need to know, Mr. Miller brings them to the action plan column (see Figure 7.4 on p. 54). Since they are familiar with the process, they quickly list the resources they should use. Mr. Miller reminds them, "Remember that we can do lab activities and we can also have demonstrations."

Once Mr. Miller thinks the students have generated the needed information, he asks the groups which issues they wish to pursue, reminding them that several groups may pursue one issue. He also reminds them that all items under learning issues should be investigated. As they choose their issues, Mr. Miller marks down in Column 3 which groups are researching what issues. Then, before they start their independent work, he

FIGURE 7.1

PBL Chart Showing Student Ideas to Educate People About Indigestion

Ideas	Facts	Learning Issues	Action Plan
Could do a demonstration for them. Get them an article to read. Could write up something for them. Tell them to buy the most expensive medication. Change their diet since the food is too rich for them. Write TV ads.			

asks each group to develop a plan and tell him about it. As they develop and share this action plan, Mr. Miller suggests ways they can further refine their strategies and offers advice on how they can begin their work.

Revisiting the Problem

After students complete their independent work, Mr. Miller asks each group to discuss how they went about their work and the information they found. They evaluate the strategies they used as well as the resources they discovered. After the groups have reported, Mr. Miller says, "Now let's look at our chart. Is there anything you want to add? Are there any additional issues which have to be looked into?" As shown in Figure 7.5, (see p. 55) students add to the facts column as well as to the learning issues column.

FIGURE 7.2

PBL Chart Showing Student Ideas and Facts About Indigestion

Ideas	Facts	Learning Issues	Action Plan
Could do a demonstration for them. Get them an article to read. Could write up something for them. Tell them to buy the most expensive medication. Change their diet since the food is too rich for them. Write TV ads.	Has upset stomach/ indigestion. Indigestion caused by stomach acid. Doctor prescribes over-the- counter medication. Prescribe antacid. Heartburn is same as acid indigestion. Antacid helps acid stomach.		

At this point the teacher says, "It seems as though we have found quite a few new facts and have come up with a number of learning issues that will require one or two more periods of research."

Mr. Miller then goes to the action plan column for additional suggestions, ultimately returning to the groups who, in turn, select issues, develop plans, and then do independent work. This process runs smoothly because the students have been working with it for quite some time. However, when Mr. Miller first started, he had to go very slowly, explain each step in detail, and, above all, limit the complexity of the problem and ensure that all the necessary research materials were available in the classroom.

When students request his help in showing how neutralizer works, Mr. Miller conducts a demonstration. He shows how combining an acid and a base neutralizes them both in a chemical reaction that yields water

Figure 7.3

PBL Chart Showing Student Ideas, Facts, and What Students Think They Should Know About Indigestion

Ideas	Facts	Learning Issues	Action Plan
Could do a demonstration for them. Get them an article to read. Could write up something for them. Tell them to buy the most expensive medication. Change their diet since the food is too rich for them. Write TV ads.	Has upset stomach/ indigestion. Indigestion caused by stomach acid. Doctor prescribes over-the- counter medication. Prescribe antacid. Heartburn is same as acid indigestion. Antacid helps acid stomach.	What is stomach acid? What is antacid? What is mean- ing of indiges- tion? How does antacid help an acid stomach? What are antacids and what's in them? What are some antacids? What is heart- burn and what causes it?	

and a salt. In this demonstration, he uses litmus paper to show the level of acidity before and after the experiment.

Now Mr. Miller says, "Our problem was to try and help family members understand what acid and antacids are and to also help them decide which over-the-counter medicine to choose to help them with their problem. Now that you have found more information about how antacids work, how can you find out the best way of determining what product to recommend?"

One student answers, "We could look at their advertisements."

Another student suggests, "We could find an article comparing them."

A third student offers, "Or we could compare them ourselves in class."

Since the students enthusiastically support doing their own compari-

FIGURE 7.4

PBL Chart Showing Student Ideas, Facts, Learning Issues, and List of Resources to Learn About Indigestion

Ideas	Facts	Learning Issues	Action Plan
Could do a demonstration for them. Get them an article to read. Could write up something for them. Tell them to buy the most expensive medication. Change their diet since the food is too rich for them. Write TV ads.	Has upset stomach/ indigestion. Indigestion caused by stomach acid. Doctor prescribes over-the-counter medication. Prescribe antacid. Heartburn is same as acid indigestion. Antacid helps acid stomach.	What is stomach acid? What is antacid? What is meaning of indigestion? How does antacid help an acid stomach? What are antacids and what's in them? What are some antacids? What is heartburn and what causes it?	Look up in textbooks. Use dictionary. Use encyclopedia. Use programs on computer. Visit a pharmacy. Call a pharmacist. Do a lab experiment. Have Mr. Miller do demonstration. Use Reference Chart from previous problems.

son, Mr. Miller asks how they could perform such an experiment. If students hadn't suggested an experiment themselves, Mr. Miller would have drawn their attention back to the first suggestion in the ideas column.

Now one student says, "We could each take a different product and see its results on us."

Mr. Miller asks, "Do you think that would be scientific? How would you measure the different effects?"

Another student answers, "We could test products in test tubes using equal amounts of acid and product."

"Excellent idea," Mr. Miller offers. "But how would you determine how well the product worked?"

"Use the same paper you used for your experiment," one student suggests.

FIGURE 7.5

PBL Chart Showing Additions in Facts and Learning Issues Columns

Ideas	Facts	Learning Issues	Action Plan
Could do a demonstration for them. Get them an article to read. Could write up something for them. Tell them to buy the most expensive medication. Change their diet since the food is too rich for them. Write TV ads.	Has upset stomach/indigestion. Indigestion caused by stomach acid. Doctor prescribes over-the-counter medication. Prescribe antacid. Heartburn is same as acid indigestion. Antacid helps acid stomach. Some medications are liquids, some are tablets, others are chewed vs. swallowed. Antacids can be bases or salt. pH measures acid. Base and acid together is called neutralizer. New research shows bacteria also causes indigestion. New treatments on the market.	What is stomach acid? What is antacid? What is meaning of indigestion? How does antacid help an acid stomach? What are antacids and what's in them? What are some antacids? What is heartburn and what causes it? Why are medicines in different forms? What are bases? What are salts? What do they contain? How does the neutralizer work? Which is the best product?	Look up in textbooks. Use dictionary. Use encyclopedia. Use programs on computer. Visit a pharmacy. Call a pharmacist. Do a lab experiment. Have Mr. Miller do demonstration. Use Reference Chart from previous problems.

"The litmus paper," offers another.

The first student agrees: "Yes, use the litmus paper, and see what antacid changes it the right color."

Mr. Miller provides the groups with samples of various antacid products, an acid with similar strength to that of an upset stomach, and an outline for the experiment based on students' comments. The students combine the acid with the antacid and measure the resulting liquid with litmus paper. The product whose combination with acid produces the most neutral liquid as measured with the litmus paper is declared to be the best.

Producing a Product or Performance

At this point Mr. Miller says, "Now that we know which product is most effective, each of you will write your own report to your family members. But before you do, you and your group should discuss what should be included in your report. Remember it should be written so it can be easily understood."

Each group meets to collaborate on outlines for the individual reports. Each group determines what research should be included and how the results of their research should be presented. Again Mr. Miller goes from group to group, monitoring their progress, making suggestions, and asking questions. Once each group has finished an outline, Mr. Miller assigns the writing of the individual reports for homework over the weekend.

Evaluating Performance and the Problem

Mr. Miller uses these reports, his daily observations, and the lab reports done by individual students to form the basis of his evaluation. He uses his notes on suggestions made in class and in groups to determine each grade. Students are evaluated for the breadth of their research, the accuracy of the information, the quality of their reasoning, and their success at developing new questions and answering old ones. The individual reports are evaluated for their accuracy, coverage of the issue, clarity, and depth of understanding. He also knows that family members will read the reports and provide their own feedback to each child.

Since Mr. Miller uses PBL throughout his curriculum, by the time students reach this lesson he evaluates their success with problem solving more strictly than he did earlier in the course. Early in the year he would have controlled the research more tightly and designed the experiment himself; now he leaves much more of the mechanics to the students to determine.

Implications for Other Teachers

Many science lessons can easily be adapted to PBL by starting with the questions scientists ask and challenging students to discover the answers rather than having the teacher present facts and perform experiments to demonstrate them. For example, a biology class can start with the question of what plants eat, leading to an investigation of photosynthesis. Or a physics class can ask why a thrown ball doesn't fall straight down, leading to questions on motion and gravity.

Teachers can use PBL to show students the role science plays in everyday life and to show the scientific process. PBL also shows students how to think as scientists. Using PBL proves to students that science is not something just found in books or performed solely by people in white lab coats. It can inspire students to become scientists themselves and increase their knowledge of scientific information, the procedures through which questions are asked and answered, and how new knowledge is discovered.

Questions to Ask Before Starting

Before starting to craft a PBL science problem, consider the following questions:

- What information should students learn?
- What investigative techniques and problem-solving abilities should students develop?
- How can this scientific information or technique be connected to real life?
- How would this project expand students' independence and ability to learn and solve problems on their own?

8 3rd Grade Social Studies Problem: "Welcoming Newcomers to Our School"

In today's urban schools, students' diverse backgrounds and personal histories create both opportunities and challenges for using problem-based learning (PBL). The absence of a common student background requires teachers to bring to the classroom stories and information from many different cultures and histories. PBL provides a way to weave these separate strands together. It also provides a structure that compels student interaction, encourages them to use primary sources, excites them to look beyond the walls of the classroom, and requires them to develop materials that demonstrate what they know and are able to do.

PBL is particularly valuable in inner-city social studies classrooms because it avoids the problem of teaching a history that some students feel is not "theirs." Problem-based learning offers students a way to incorporate their current knowledge and interests with what they are learning in the school's curriculum.

Marsha Williams is an elementary teacher in an inner-city neighborhood that is predominantly African American and Afro-Caribbean American. She uses PBL to engage her students and to link her course material to their lives. Many of her school's 600 students are first-generation Americans or new immigrants from more than 25 different countries. Consequently, her register is in a constant state of flux with new students added and removed throughout the year. In December one year, her 3rd grade classroom had 26 students, and two new arrivals were expected the following month, one from Jamaica and one from Kenya.

By using PBL, Ms. Williams meets several of the objectives in her social studies and language arts curriculum guides. She also responds to the personal needs of the children. Her lesson builds on their interest in their own backgrounds as well as on their common experiences of being "the new student." She uses PBL to give her heterogeneous class a chance to fully participate in the learning experience, to develop their abilities to learn on their own, and to direct their own activities. This is especially important in urban schools where students have a great range of skill levels and academic orientations.

Connecting with the Problem

Before presenting a problem statement that defines the task, Ms. Williams gently leads the children into the situation behind the problem, trying in as many ways as possible to have students connect with the assignment. She knows that her students will not put forth their full effort just because the teacher has given instructions. Instead, she makes the problem seem more interesting by relating it to their lives and interests, knowing that the more emotional energy and commitment her students invest in the problem, the more they will learn from it.

For example, she might have her students recall their feelings the first day they came to a new school: "How many of you here have changed schools? What did it feel like to be a stranger, without any friends in a class where everyone knows each other? Now imagine what it would be like to do this in a strange country, in a different language from what you've always known. Some of you here did this, moving to this school from a different country. How did this make you feel?"

Once a connection has been established, Ms. Williams is ready to present students with the problem statement:

> Each year, our school has many children arriving from foreign countries. Often they have a difficult time fitting in. This year, the principal has formed a group to help make these newly arrived children feel welcome. In our class, new children will come from the countries of Jamaica and Kenya. What do you

think the school can do to make these children feel welcome? What suggestions can our class make to the principal? How will we present our suggestions?

This problem has three aspects that will interest the students. First, it is an experience that happens in their own world. At one time or another, they all have been new students or been in a class with a new student. Second, it has a practical component. Their class will be welcoming these new students, and their suggestions from this problem will affect the newcomers' adjustment to the school. Finally, the countries they study through this problem will be more real to them than other far-off lands since their future classmates are coming from these places.

Once the problem has been presented, Ms. Williams makes it clear to the children that they will work in groups and individually. In addition, she points out that after she and the class have evaluated the results, the suggestions will actually be presented to the principal and used to help the two new students. This is not an exercise done just for the teacher to grade; it is something real that will affect someone else's life.

Setting Up the Structure

Ms. Williams next explains to the children how they are going to work. She tells them that she will put up sheets of newsprint on which she will record their work. Since this is the 3rd grade and she does not want students' difficulties with writing to slow down the flow of ideas, Ms. Williams has decided to act as recorder for the class.

She tells them, "Boys and girls, now that we know what our problem is, we have to think up possible solutions for it. I will use these large sheets of paper to record our thoughts as we try to find a solution. I will divide the paper into four columns.

"I will call the first column 'Ideas.' In this column I will record any ideas you have right now about solving the problem. In the second column is what we know about the problem. I will record whatever facts we know. Many of you will have a great deal to contribute to this column. In the third column we will list what we need to know to help us come up with a solution. The last column is what we will do to gather information. There we will list the ways we are going to gather this information and solve the problem. This will be our plan of action."

Ms. Williams explains to the children that they will go through each of the first three columns. When they are finished, they then will be given time to work independently or in small groups. Figure 8.1 shows the chart the class will complete.

FIGURE 8.1

Headings for the PBL Chart for Ms. Williams's 3rd Grade Class

Ideas	What We Know	What We Need to Know	What We Will Do to Gather Information

---

Visiting the Problem

Now that Ms. Williams has set up the way the class will work, she guides students to think through the problem. She reads the problem with the children, then asks, "Do any of you have ideas about how we could help these newcomers?"

She then records students' ideas in the first column. In this first stage she does not pass judgment on the usefulness of their suggestions; instead, she encourages everyone to participate. The ideas column ends up looking like Figure 8.2 (see p. 62).

As soon as she believes the class has exhausted all the ideas they can think of, Ms. Williams goes on to the second column and asks, "What do we know about this problem? What information or facts do we have that will help us?" She then records these student responses in the second column, displayed in Figure 8.3 (see p. 63).

Once the children have finished sharing the information they think will contribute to solving the problem, Ms. Williams asks, "What else do

FIGURE 8.2

PBL Chart Showing Student Ideas to Welcome Two New Students to the School

Ideas	What We Know	What We Need to Know	What We Will Do to Gather Information
Have a welcome party. Write a book about our school. Make a club. Ask children for ideas.			

we need to know to help us arrive at a solution?" She fills in the third column with the students' proposals, as shown in Figure 8.4 (see p. 64).

After she has finished writing, she asks the children to look over her notes to see if there is anything more they wish to add. When the children are satisfied, Ms. Williams points to the last column and says, "Now we need to decide how we are going to find out what we need to know. Let's look at our list and decide who wants to work on certain topics."

The teacher and her students look over the list. They review it and decide who will work on which topics. They also decide which resources they will use. The teacher recognizes that by allowing the children to choose with whom they wish to work and on what they wish to work, she is ensuring a greater commitment to gathering the needed information. She knows that placing these decisions in the hands of students is a risk, but helping students feel ownership of the project will reduce discipline problems and increase their interest through long periods of time.

Before she works with the children on self-directed learning, Ms. Williams makes sure they recognize the variety of resources available to them and how to use those resources effectively. She knows that her students tend to rely on text material, so she encourages them to explore other resources. She reminds them that they might find useful information from

FIGURE 8.3

PBL Chart Showing Student Ideas and Facts About Welcoming Two New Students to the School

Ideas	What We Know	What We Need to Know	What We Will Do to Gather Information
Have a welcome party. Write a book about our school. Make a club. Ask children for ideas.	Kenya is in Africa Jamaica is an island. Many children in our school come from Jamaica. One of our teachers comes from Africa. Many of our teachers come from the Caribbean. Some children from other places have difficulty.		

the library computers, magazines, other newcomers to the school, teachers, other staff members, and community members. Once she has completed this review, she asks the students to commit to one of the items in the what-we-need-to-know column and to say how they will research that area.

Ms. Williams meets with each group to go over ways of working for the next few days. The children then begin their self-directed study using the resources in the classroom and library. While Ms. Williams provides guidance and support, reminding them of the problem and reigning them in when they stray too far from the topic, the students take the lead in determining what and how they will investigate. In this case, the students

FIGURE 8.4

PBL Chart Showing Student Ideas, Facts, and What Students Think They Should Know About the Two New Students

Ideas	What We Know	What We Need to Know	What We Will Do to Gather Information
Have a welcome party. Write a book about our school. Make a club. Ask children for ideas.	Kenya is in Africa. Jamaica is an island. Many children in our school come from Jamaica. One of our teachers comes from Africa. Many of our teachers come from the Caribbean. Some children from other places have difficulty.	Schools in Kenya. Schools in Jamaica. Facts about Jamaica and Kenya. How children from these places feel about our school.	

choose to interview other new students in the school about their experiences. They read encyclopedia articles and appropriate magazines. They investigate the games people play in Kenya and Jamaica, the foods people eat in those countries, and what children learn in their schools.

Revisiting the Problem

When the children have completed their research, Ms. Williams asks them to talk about the resources they used. She asks them to speak about how they used the resources and the ease or difficulty they had with each one. She knows this will help all her students in the future. She recognizes that her students will have problems with depth and accuracy of sources because they are only 3rd graders and this is their first time doing self-directed research. However, she sees this as a start, building experience for longer projects later in the year.

Once the evaluation of resources is completed, Ms. Williams returns the class to the problem and the chart by saying, "Let's look at some of the ideas you had in Column 1 and see if we want to keep them up there." She then goes to Column 2 to see if students have any facts that need to be changed or added. In Column 3 they consider any additional information that should be researched. If so, an additional period of self-directed study will be scheduled. If not, she then says to the students, "What suggestions will our class make? How will we present our suggestions?" The class then decides on the list of suggestions and the format for making them.

Producing a Product or Performance

In this case, the suggestions are presented in the form of an illustrated book to be made available to all new children. Their own class will have booklets called "Life in Kenya" and "Life in Jamaica," which they will create with information from their research. The class also makes a list of recommendations to the principal including assigning buddies to new students, providing teachers with information about the culture of the countries where their students are from, and inviting parents and older children from other countries to talk to the class about their experiences.

Evaluating Performance and the Problem

Both the teacher and the students will evaluate the project. Ms. Williams has designed a very simple assessment procedure. She first evaluates herself as the facilitator of PBL in her 3rd grade classroom. Next she evaluates the PBL lesson: both the process and the content. Finally, the children are asked to evaluate their own performance with the PBL process.

Although Ms. Williams knew about PBL's effectiveness, she still was surprised that her students were so involved in solving the problem and that they were really interested in what they were doing. She reported less of a need to supervise students' investigations and a marked decrease in disciplinary actions. Since this was her first time using PBL, she discovered the importance of preparation and organization, which is key to making PBL lessons work. She had to notify the library to make sure that all the right resources would be available and laid out. She also learned that she had to alert everyone her students would contact and convince them to cooperate.

Classroom Atmosphere

Such an interactive lesson would not work effectively without first creating an atmosphere in which children felt comfortable taking risks, where they could readily admit that they are unfamiliar with something and are willing to explore to learn something new. In Ms. Williams's classroom, she has created an environment where her students can speculate about solutions to problems and where a variety of opinions is valued.

Ms. Williams created this nonthreatening classroom by encouraging everyone to participate and by valuing student responses, even those that are not the desired answer. Instead of asking all the questions and demanding that students instantly produce a correct answer, she encourages them to ask questions, think through a problem to develop an answer, and even make mistakes if it will bring the class closer to finding a solution. She asks opinion questions that force students to think but do not have a right answer, asking "why?" and "what do you mean by that statement?" Finally, she has redefined the relationships in her class so that they are student centered, with students asking each other questions and seeing all of the members of the class as possible sources of valuable information.

Further Work

Now that students are familiar with PBL and how to use the school's resources, Ms. Williams can extend it further. She can have her students construct a guide to the community for the newcomers, which would require comparisons between their countries and the United States. She can have her students research the holidays in both countries and then plan a party celebrating those traditions. Or, Ms. Williams can use PBL for a totally different topic.

Implications for Other Teachers

PBL lends itself to research-oriented projects that produce concrete products or specific actions. PBL fits very well into a social studies unit, going beyond the textbook with a wide range of possibilities for both the problem and the product. Students can compare countries, study local government by taking action on an issue, research their family backgrounds, learn about the U.S. Constitution by writing a school constitution, show an understanding of a historical period by writing a play and performing it with historically accurate costumes, or any one of many other activities.

Questions to Ask Before Starting

Before creating a social studies PBL problem, consider the following questions:

- What issues concern students in my school?
- What areas of my curriculum do students have the most difficulty understanding?
- What product would best demonstrate students' comprehension of this issue or event?
- What project could develop students' independence and willingness to learn on their own? (The problem should be challenging enough to require the students to stretch to accomplish it but should not be impossible for their skills.)

9 7th Grade Mathematics Problem: "Let's Build a Playground"

Many mathematics teachers think they already are teaching through problem-based learning (PBL). After all, math class usually involves hands-on activities where students solve math problems with pencil and paper. However, math classes often are organized so that the teacher presents a new mathematical concept, shows students how to use it, and assigns questions that require the student to use the concept to find the answers. Students rarely are given a chance to figure out the concept on their own or to work through the steps to determine how to use the concept. Instead of actively solving the problem, students answer the question by passively following the teacher's model.

The use of problem solving in mathematics has been endorsed by the National Council of Teachers of Mathematics (NCTM), whose very first standard in their *Curriculum and Evaluation Standards for School Mathematics* is "Mathematics as Problem Solving." In particular, the national standards for grades 5-8 state:

> [T]he mathematics curriculum should include numerous and varied experiences with problem solving as a method of inquiry and application so that students can:
> • use problem-solving approaches to investigate and understand mathematical content;

- formulate problems from situations within and outside mathematics;
- develop and apply a variety of strategies to solve problems, with emphasis on multistep, nonroutine problems;
- verify and interpret results with respect to the original problem situation;
- generalize solutions and strategies to new problem situations; and
- acquire confidence in using mathematics meaningfully (National Council of Teachers of Mathematics 1994, p. 75).

Rose Carlin, a seven-year veteran, is one of a growing number of teachers who has begun to incorporate these standards into her teaching. Her large middle school has 1,000 students in grades 6, 7, and 8; three-fourths are Hispanic, and one-quarter are African American.

Connecting with the Problem

Over the past decade, the apartment houses around Rose Carlin's school have been rehabilitated, attracting many new families with young children. This influx of students has necessitated the construction of a new elementary school close to her middle school. All of her students have seen the construction start on this new building, and many have younger siblings in overcrowded schools who will attend the new school.

Ms. Carlin has developed a unit that links mathematical concepts to students' interest in the construction of this new school. She starts the first lesson by asking students if they have any thoughts about the new elementary school or suggestions for what the school should include. She points out, "Have you noticed that it's going to be quite different from most of the elementary schools in this area? The building will have a different design, and the playground will have a large area. What do you think the school will be like? Do you have any suggestions for what it should include?"

The children discuss the school. They speculate about what the school will be like inside, including special rooms like the gym and cafeteria.

Ms. Carlin asks, "What about the playground? What do you think that will be like? Should it be different from the one in your own elementary school? How do you think it will be different? How can they design one playground that can be used by both small kindergartners and larger 5th graders?"

The students then relate their own experiences with playgrounds. Since many of them have attended different schools, they are able to share a variety of experiences and contribute many ideas about how playgrounds differ from school to school. Ms. Carlin tells them, "Well, class, as you can see, we've all had different experiences with playgrounds. We also have many ideas as to what playgrounds should have. Why don't we put all our knowledge and our experience to work by helping to design a model playground for the new school?" She then presents the problem:

> A new elementary school is being constructed next to our middle school. It will house approximately 600 children, kindergarten through grade 5. The cost of the school is going to be $3 million, of which 7.5 percent is set aside for the construction of the playground. Your job is to present the builders with a number of playground designs making sure you stay within the budget and also making sure that the playground accommodates children in kindergarten through grade 5.

Ms. Carlin has designed the problem to meet the NCTM standards for problem solving and to incorporate real-world concerns for budgeting and planning. The connection to the playground sparks student interest, and the idea of helping the district build a school lends a sense of immediacy to the project.

Setting Up the Structure

Ms. Carlin explains that as their final project, students will construct models of proposed playground designs and write out estimates of proposed costs. However, before they begin creating models, they must go through a series of steps to define the problem, gather information, and arrive at the solutions.

Ms. Carlin tells the students, "I'm going to put up this large piece of paper in the front of the room and divide it into four columns. The first column will be for ideas that we have about the problem. The second column will be for facts we know about the problem. The third column will be for learning issues, or things we want to know about. In the last column we will list a plan of action. This is what we will do to get the information we need."

Visiting the Problem

Ms. Carlin divides the class into problem-solving teams and assigns one student in each group to keep notes. She then asks two students to come to the front and act as recorders for the whole-class discussion. Next she suggests that they read the problem again. When that is complete, Ms. Carlin suggests, "Let's start with the first column. Do we have any ideas about how to solve this problem? Remember these are just suggestions that we can change later as we find new information."

The two students at the front record responses on the large sheet of paper (Figure 9.1), and students also take notes for their individual groups.

When Ms. Carlin believes the students have expressed all of their ideas, she goes on to the next column (see Figure 9.2 on p. 72). "What are the facts we already know?" she asks. "Let's list them."

FIGURE 9.1

PBL Chart Showing Student Ideas to Design a Playground

Ideas	Facts	Learning Issues	Action Plan
Hire someone to do it. Go to other schools that have the same playground. Put in every-thing we like to do.			

FIGURE 9.2

PBL Chart Showing Student Ideas and Facts About a Playground Design

Ideas	Facts	Learning Issues	Action Plan
Hire someone to do it. Go to other schools that have the same playground. Put in everything we like to do.	600 children. Kindergarten through grade 5. 7.5 percent of $3 million. Have to make a model.		

Ms. Carlin is paying close attention to the list as students generate it. When someone contributes the "fact" of "small space," she asks, "Charles, you've said 'small space' is a fact. Do you know for sure the playground is a small space?"

"No, not really," Charles answers.

"Do you think we would want to find out how big or small the space is?" Ms. Carlin asks.

"Yes."

"Since we want to find out this information, in what column should we write 'small space'?"

"In the learning issues column," Charles replies.

Ms. Carlin explains that as they go along, items can be placed in a number of different columns. Then she asks one student to read what they've already put on the chart. When the student is finished, Ms. Carlin point outs, "Let's look at the third column, learning issues. This is where we list what we need to know to help us with our problem. Let's list what we need to know. We already have one item up there: size of space." Figure 9.3 (see p. 73) shows how the class filled in the learning issues column.

Once the students have exhausted their suggestions, Ms. Carlin asks them to focus on the last column: "Let's look at what our action plans are going to be. What are some of your thoughts?"

FIGURE 9.3

PBL Chart Showing Student Ideas, Facts, and What Students Think They Should Know to Design a Playground

Ideas	Facts	Learning Issues	Action Plan
Hire someone to do it. Go to other schools that have the same playground. Put in every- thing we like to do.	600 children. Kindergarten through grade 5. 7.5 percent of $3 million. Have to make a model.	Size of space. Games played by children. Regulations. Safety issues. Equipment. Other play- grounds. Costs. Best way of presenting. Whom should we present to?	

One student offers, "How about size of space? How will we go about finding out about that?"

"We could go and measure it," another student suggests.

"Are there blueprints somewhere?" asks another classmate. "We could look at them."

When this is recorded, Ms. Carlin continues, "Let's take another one: 'Games played by children.' How could we find out about that?"

"We could ask them," suggests one student.

"How would you go about that?" Ms. Carlin queries.

Another student answers, "Some of us could go to an elementary school and ask."

"That's a good idea. But how can you ask so that everyone who asks will gather similar information?" Ms. Carlin presses.

"We could write down a list of questions," suggests another student.

"Brilliant!" Ms. Carlin exclaims. "What do we call it when we have a list of questions to ask and answers to select from? You sometimes see them on TV news, especially near an election."

"You mean a survey?" offers one student.

"Exactly! And you could also ask the 6th graders here if they remember what they liked to do on the playground when they were in elementary school."

As students offer additional suggestions for action plans, the recorders write them in the fourth column (see Figure 9.4).

FIGURE 9.4

PBL Chart Showing Student Ideas, Facts, Learning Issues, and Action Plans to Learn About Designing a Playground

Ideas	Facts	Learning Issues	Action Plan
Hire someone to do it. Go to other schools that have the same playground. Put in everything we like to do.	600 children. Kindergarten through grade 5. 7.5 percent of $3 million. Have to make a model.	Size of space. Games played by children. Regulations. Safety issues. Equipment. Other playgrounds. Costs. Best way of presenting. Whom should we present to?	Survey elementary children about games. Contact persons building school to find out space. Call health department about regulations. Find equipment store to get prices. Call specialist about safety. Visit other schools and take photos.

After completing the last column, Ms. Carlin has the students meet in their working groups. She tells them that each group will research the issues and design their own model. She then says, "Let's go back to our learning issues. Group 1, which issue do you want to find out about?" Each group takes turns selecting issues until none is left.

Then Ms. Carlin suggests, "Now discuss what your plan of action is going to be. How will you research your issue?" She then makes sure that the groups know that some learning issues may be selected by more than one group, but all issues should be looked into. She also makes sure that each group has a clear plan of action before the students start independent work.

Ms. Carlin has prepared the principals, librarian, resource people, and other teachers who might be contacted by the students. She has asked for permission for her students to enter an elementary school and survey their students. Most important, she has made sure that whatever resources the students will need in the classroom are readily available. She knows that for a PBL problem to be effective, the bulk of the teacher's job is the planning and preparation before the students begin work.

Revisiting the Problem

Students perform their research, surveying elementary school students and 6th graders for their playground preferences, calling playground supply stores for prices, checking with the city government for safety regulations, and calculating the area of the playground by measuring its length and width. After completing their independent work in the specific time allotment given to them by Ms. Carlin, the students gather to share their information. Ms. Carlin begins by suggesting, "Let's hear from each of the groups about what they learned and how they went about gathering their information. Some groups worked together while others paired up in teams."

Each group talks about its work. Ms. Carlin is particularly interested in having students clearly express the steps they went through as well as the difficulties they had. By sharing their process, each group acts as a teacher to the other students, showing the different ways of solving problems. Once each group has reported—over several periods—Ms. Carlin then says, "Let's look at the columns to see whether we want to add or delete any information and also to see if we need to do any more research before we begin to make our models and create our budgets."

She asks the group that conducted the student survey to read the results to the class. When they are finished, she probes, "Do we have all the information we need to make a playground based on the survey?" After the students have raised additional questions, Ms. Carlin adds, "I'm sure you know that the workers who are building the new school have to be paid, too. We need to find out how much they charge per hour and include this in our budget. So, we need to make sure we know how long it takes to install each piece of equipment we buy. Also, our safety group learned that we will need wood chips under any climbing equipment. You will have to calculate how much we will need depending on your area and how much that will cost. Similarly, if you want a hard surface to play kickball or hopscotch you will need to calculate how much asphalt you will need and its costs."

The students return to the library or telephone for additional research to answer the new questions and to find out the costs of workers, asphalt, and wood chips.

Producing a Product or Performance

After the additional research is gathered and shared, Ms. Carlin suggests, "Now that we have gathered all of the information we need, let's review what we should focus on when creating our model playground and the budget."

One student offers, "We know what kids like to do on playgrounds, little kids and big kids."

"And we know how much space we have," suggests another.

A third student points out, "We know about equipment and how much it costs."

The students continue generating the list of what they know to help them plan. When Ms. Carlin determines that all the information they need has been listed, she says, "It's time now to plan your model. Look back to the survey and see what games students play and what equipment they need. Then look at your costs to see how you can satisfy the largest percentage of students while staying in your budget."

She continues, "To do this, first determine your budget. You have 7.5 percent of $3 million. Then go back to the survey and determine what percentage of the students would use each piece of equipment. Then look at the costs for the various items you need and determine how many of each you can afford. Remember, we will be presenting this to the school board's building committee so you will have to show how your plan would meet the students' needs and stay within the budget."

Finally she says, "After you have made your plan, you can build a model. I've laid out all of the materials and supplies you will need at the back of the room. Each group should have one person gather what is needed. If additional material is needed, that person should speak to me. Remember that the model should be proportional to the real playground. Does anyone know what *proportional* means?"

"The right numbers?" offers one student.

"Very close." Ms. Carlin then asks a student to look up the definition of *proportional* in the dictionary and read it to the class. Then Ms. Carlin paraphrases: "Building it proportionately means using the same scale throughout your model. If the real length of the playground is 50 feet but your model is 10 inches wide, what scale are you using?"

After a moment one student answers, "One inch for every five feet."

"So if the jungle gym is 10 feet on the playground, how big should it be on your model?"

"Two inches," answers another student.

"Very good. By staying with the same proportions you will be able to see if someone on the swings would hit someone on the seesaw, or if the hopscotch area is too close to the jumprope court." Ms. Carlin then tells students how many periods they will have to come up with a design and how they will present it to the whole class at the end of that time.

As the students work, Ms. Carlin goes from group to group, checking their math and their plans. If a group's plan seems to have too much of one type of equipment, she brings their attention back to the survey and asks if they think their mix of equipment would satisfy the greatest number of students.

Before the groups began their plans and their models, Ms. Carlin had them write letters to invite members of the school board's building committee to their presentations. She also suggests that students invite the building's designer and the principal of the new school. In these presentations, each group has 15 minutes to explain its vision for the playground, how it will meet the needs of elementary school students, and the mathematical calculations they performed in designing the plan and the model.

Evaluating Performance and the Problem

Ms. Carlin has created this problem in light of the NCTM standards urging increased attention be given to "developing problem situations that require the application of a number of mathematical ideas" and to "using multiple assessment techniques, including written, oral, and demonstration formats" (National Council of Teachers of Mathematics 1994). She therefore evaluates her students on (1) their ability to recognize the need for mathematics to solve problems and (2) the quality and accuracy of their work. Students' attention to the budget and to proper proportions in their model also are considered. Through observation of students' day-to-day work and their final products, Ms. Carlin gains a clear picture of the students' areas of strength and weakness and plans for follow-up accordingly.

Implications for Other Teachers

While the building of a new elementary school provided Ms. Carlin with an immediate hook to catch students' attention, this lesson could be adapted to proposals for a new park, modifications to a current playground, or ways to better use the school gym.

Problem-based learning can be incorporated into other types of mathematics lessons as well. Students could perform experiments to discover the laws of probability and determine if they should advise their parents to enter the lottery. They could plan a trip across the United States, calculating where they would stop each night according to how far they could travel and how much it would cost at current gasoline prices. Students in geometry could design a new container for soft drinks, calculating which shape would require the least material to make (smallest surface area) while holding the greatest amount of liquid (high volume).

Questions to Ask Before Starting

Before beginning a PBL lesson for mathematics, consider the following questions:

- What mathematical principals would this lesson require students to develop or enhance?
- How does the lesson reflect the NCTM standards?
- How will this lesson show students how to use mathematical thinking in the real world?

10 9th Grade Biology Problem: "Food, Glorious Food"

Anyone who has ever walked through a school cafeteria or seen teenagers eat knows of their interest in food and their lack of concern for nutrition. In part, this is because students do not understand the value of nutrition and the effects of unhealthy food. Lucille Lambert, a science teacher who has taught in her comprehensive city high school for more than a decade, knows that most teenagers are completely unconcerned with nutrition and eat many fatty foods. So she has constructed a problem-based learning (PBL) lesson centered around improving school lunches as a way of showing students how to practice better nutrition.

Connecting with the Problem

Ms. Lambert begins one of her 9th grade biology classes by reading from several newspaper accounts that detail the conditions of food handling in schools. She also shows a brief clip from a television news exposé about school food. She knows this will stimulate a great deal of discussion since students always complain about cafeteria food and have strong opinions about what they are willing to eat.

She attempts to guide the discussion so that it will be more constructive by asking students, "Can you remember if you ever had school lunches that you thought were good?" Most students say they can't. However, several say they can, and Ms. Lambert invites those students to describe the food for the class.

One student answers, "When I was in elementary school they used to have food like I ate at home."

"What do you mean by that?" Ms. Lambert probes.

"Well, our school had a big kitchen and the cooks used to come from our own neighborhood and they knew what we liked to eat."

Another student offers, "I liked the food when we had pizza or good hot dogs or hamburgers like you get at McDonald's or Burger King."

Ms. Lambert lets the discussion continue, then offers, "Most of you agree that the food in school cafeterias is not to your liking, but a few of you have had good cafeteria food. Why don't we try to come up with some suggestions and see if we can change things?" Now she presents the problem statement:

> Recent newspaper and television stories have reported that school lunch programs are neither healthy for students nor economical for schools. The school board has asked for proposals for a new lunch system. This is your opportunity to tell the board how students think school lunches should be improved.

Setting Up the Structure

Since Ms. Lambert has used PBL with this class, she does not spend a great deal of time setting up the ground rules. She does reemphasize the need for students to listen to one another and also the need to pay close attention to what is being written by the recorder.

She tells students, "We are all familiar with the system for planning our problem solving. Remember, the first column is for ideas that we have about the problem. The second column will be for facts, things we know about the problem. The third will be for learning issues, what we need to know to help us arrive at solutions. The fourth column, action plan, describes how we are going to go about finding the information we need to arrive at possible solutions. Also, sometimes a person will suggest an idea for one column that really belongs in a different column. If this happens we simply will write the comment in the proper spot. May I have two volunteers to write down our thoughts?"

Visiting the Problem

While two students come to the front of the room to act as recorders, Ms. Lambert organizes the other students into groups. One person in each group is designated to copy the recorders' chart and to keep notes.

Next Ms. Lambert asks someone to read the problem. Then she suggests, "Let's write up some ideas we have about this. What should our cafeteria do?" The students at the front of the room and the recorders at the desks take notes, as in Figure 10.1.

When Ms. Lambert decides her students have put up all of their ideas for improvements, she has them go on to the facts column. She tells them, "To solve this problem, we need to show that our plan for school lunches provides better nutrition at a lower cost than the existing plan. What do we know about school lunches?" This information goes in Column 2, as shown in Figure 10.2 (see p. 82). However, during the discussion, Ms. Lambert presses students about whether or not certain pieces of information are actually facts.

FIGURE 10.1

PBL Chart Showing Student Ideas to Improve School Lunches

Ideas	Facts	Learning Issues	Action Plan
Serve more burgers. Chinese food. Hire McDonald's or Taco Bell. Burger King. Give students more choices. Hire neighborhood cooks who know what we eat. Set up a food court.			

FIGURE 10.2

PBL Chart Showing Student Ideas, Facts, and Learning Issues About School Lunches

Ideas	Facts	Learning Issues	Action Plan
Serve more burgers. Chinese food. Hire McDonald's or Taco Bell. Burger King. Give students more choices. Hire neighborhood cooks who know what we eat. Set up a food court.	Students don't like most food. Some foods are better than others. Many people eat the school lunch every day. The government pays for some students' lunches.	Are the lunches healthy? Are the lunches economical?	

When someone suggests the fact "not healthy," Ms. Lambert asks, "What do you mean by *healthy*?" After the students offer some answers, Ms. Lambert probes, "Do we know for a fact that school lunches are not healthy? Is something a fact just because the media reports it?" When students shake their heads or say no, Ms. Lambert asks, "Then should it go in the learning issues column so we can find out more about it?" Ms. Lambert does the same when someone says that the lunches are "not economical." As Figure 10.2 shows, these queries end up in the learning issues, not facts, column.

After all known facts are listed, Ms. Lambert says, "Let's look at what we need to know to come up with some possible solutions." These learning issues are listed in Figure 10.3 (see p. 83). She has anticipated that because of her students' prior knowledge, they will generate issues such as food categories, the USDA food pyramid, and calories. She has charts and glossaries ready for the groups of students when they begin their independent work.

FIGURE 10.3

PBL Chart Showing Student Ideas, Facts, and What Students Think They Should Know to Improve School Lunches

Ideas	Facts	Learning Issues	Action Plan
Serve more burgers. Chinese food. Hire McDonald's or Taco Bell. Burger King. Give students more choices. Hire neighborhood cooks who know what we eat. Set up a food court.	Students don't like most food. Some foods are better than others. Many people eat the school lunch every day. The government pays for some students' lunches.	Are the lunches healthy? What do they need to be more healthy? Are the lunches economical? How much should they cost? How much do we have to eat? How many calories do we need? What foods are better than others? Food pyramid. Are there studies on nutritional content of foods?	

Once the students have generated ideas, listed facts, and determined their learning issues, Ms. Lambert asks, "Could someone, without looking at the board or the notes at their table, summarize what we've put up?"

If no one person volunteers, she asks if a group will volunteer. Once a summary has been provided, Ms. Lambert says, "Let's look at the first column. These are some ideas that we have for healthier and more economical lunches. What I'd like each group to do is to choose one or two that they think might be the best alternatives."

Each group chooses an idea. In case two groups choose the same one, Ms. Lambert arbitrates. Then Ms. Lambert says to each group, "Now that you have chosen an idea, each group should decide what learning issues it is going to choose and what the action plan will be."

She reminds them of their task: to look into the nutritional and economical factors related to their choice for a solution. Once each group has a plan of action prepared, she has them share it with the class, as in Figure 10.4.

FIGURE 10.4

PBL Chart Showing Student Ideas, Facts, Learning Issues, and Action Plans to Learn About Improving School Lunches

Ideas	Facts	Learning Issues	Action Plan
Serve more burgers. Chinese food. Hire McDonald's or Taco Bell. Burger King. Give students more choices. Hire neighborhood cooks who know what we eat. Set up a food court.	Students don't like most food. Some foods are better than others. Many people eat the school lunch every day. The government pays for some students' lunches.	Are the lunches healthy? What do they need to be more healthy? Are the lunches economical? How much should they cost? How much do we have to eat? How many calories do we need? What foods are better than others? Food pyramid. Are there studies on nutritional content of foods?	Go to food places and get menus. Get prices of foods from cafeteria and outside sources. Check calories. Check meals on food pyramid. Check calories needed by teenagers. Make charts comparing information. Speak to nutritionist. Speak to doctors. Read some books. Survey students. Speak to school cooks and dieticians.

Revisiting the Problem

Each group chooses the areas it wishes to investigate and is given a set number of periods to complete work. Ms. Lambert monitors each group's progress, making suggestions and clearing the way with librarians and other school staff members. When one group decides to interview cafeteria cooks and workers, Ms. Lambert arranges a class visit to the cafeteria so workers can be interviewed without interrupting their jobs. Another group visits fast-food restaurants after school to obtain information on the nutritional value of their food.

When the investigations are complete, Ms. Lambert asks each of the groups to report on what they found and how their research was done, making sure that all groups gain the benefit of everyone's information and research techniques.

After each group has an opportunity to share, she says, "Now we must determine what to recommend to the board of education. Let's have each group tell us the idea they chose and then tell us if they want to stick with it now that they have done their research. We will also want to find out if they want to add to the facts column or if there are any learning issues that still have to be researched. Remember, for the final presentation you will need to be able to prove that your solution offers the most nutrition and least fat content for the lowest possible price."

Each group returns to the ideas column to see if members wish to stay with the solution they originally investigated. They then add to or delete from the other columns according to the information they found. Next they return to their research to answer the additional questions necessary to evaluate their solutions.

In the final step of the project, the teacher demonstrates how to measure the calories in a gram of food by burning the food under a test tube of water and measuring the temperature change. She performs additional experiments to find the fat content and nutritional value of the food. Each group is given the necessary apparatus and told to analyze the calories and fat content in food from their solution. The group that recommended hiring McDonald's to run the cafeteria tests a piece of a burger while the group that suggested using local cooks analyzes part of a home-cooked meal. These are contrasted with measurements from part of a typical school lunch.

Producing a Product or Performance

At this point Ms. Lambert offers, "We have gathered all of the information—now we have to share it. What each group will do now is create a presentation for the class. This will let us see which of the group's selections will have the greatest nutritional value and be the most economical for the school."

Each group takes its proposed solution from the first column or additional solutions that emerged from research and develops a presentation for why their plan would provide better nutrition, greater student approval, and more economical lunches. They show how these foods would meet students' nutritional needs and where the meals would fit on the food pyramid. Students compare these results with a nutritional analysis of recent cafeteria meals. Each group also develops a sample week's menus showing the calories, fat, and nutrition for each dollar spent on food.

Students are given several periods to prepare their presentations; another period is spent on their reports. One group develops a presentation on the computer; another group performs the calorie experiment as part of its exhibition; and a third group develops detailed charts showing the effect of these foods on the human body. After each presentation, other groups question the presenters on the benefits of each plan. After each group has made its presentation, the class votes on which presentation should be offered to the board of education.

Evaluating Performance and the Problem

Ms. Lambert evaluates students throughout the project. First, she collects the action plans the groups write before they start their research and determines if they will cover all the necessary elements. She observes students throughout the research stage and evaluates their level of participation and the thoroughness of their research. Finally, she evaluates their presentation, checking to make sure they understand the concept of proper nutrition and can correctly compare their proposed solution to what's currently served in the cafeteria. In the past, she has used pre- and post-tests to determine mastery of content, but by evaluating their PBL project she can measure both their knowledge of content and their ability to use that knowledge in real-world activities.

Follow-Up Activities

To continue the project, students could compare the foods and health of different cultures to see the relationship between diet and national characteristics. Students could evaluate the foods served most often in their own homes and suggest substitutions to make the meals healthier. They could construct a cookbook of healthy recipes with nutritional analyses and pictograms of where the recipe fits into the food pyramid. In addition, students could keep a food diary of what they eat each day and analyze the number of calories they take in and the food's nutritional value.

Working with the social studies or civic teachers, students could trace the origins of foods used in the school and the USDA policies that ship food around the United States. Students could also investigate why certain foods are healthier for humans than other foods and compare what humans eat to foods eaten by other animals. Why did humans evolve to eat these foods? Why might a taste for sweets and fats have been helpful in earlier periods of history?

11 5th Grade Interdisciplinary Problem: "Why Can't We Play?"

Problems often grow out of an existing school curriculum. A history teacher might ask students to research air-raid drills of the 1950s and develop a plan for their own school, or an English teacher might ask her class to make a presentation to the English teachers on whether *Huckleberry Finn* should remain in the curriculum. These problems have very clear content and skill objectives and could be planned well in advance. However, teachers also should be alert to problems that emerge from students' day-to-day experiences. For example, Daniel Lopez used problem-based learning (PBL) with his 5th grade students in a large K–8 school in a very poor neighborhood to solve a problem the children themselves brought to his attention.

Connecting with the Problem

After hearing his 5th grade students complain that the older children wouldn't let them play basketball during their shared recess, Mr. Lopez decided to use this issue to introduce his class to problem-based learning. Students were instantly connected to the problem since it emerged from their own lives, and they knew they would benefit from resolving the situation. Mr. Lopez restated the problem for them as follows:

Several 5th and 6th graders have complained that the bigger children on the playground will not allow them to use the basketball area. How can we fix this situation so that anyone who wishes to do so can play basketball?

Setting Up the Structure

Because Mr. Lopez has not used PBL with his students before this, he has to explain what PBL is and how the class will use the PBL process to solve the problem. He tells them, "To help us solve our basketball problem, we are all going to do something different over the next couple of days. I'm going to put up this paper on the bulletin board at the back of the room, and I'll divide it into four columns. In the first column, I'm going to write down ideas you have about how we might solve the problem. In the second column I will write down any facts we know about the problem. In the third column, I will write down the things we need to find out to help solve the problem. And in the fourth column I will write down what we are going to do to find out more information."

Mr. Lopez then explains the difference between ideas and facts as well as questions and resources so students understand what information they should put into each column. Because many of his students have difficulties with reading and writing, Mr. Lopez opts to act as the recorder for the class. He also has decided to devote only four or five class periods to this project because of the real-life need to resolve it quickly.

Visiting the Problem

Mr. Lopez asks if someone would read the problem. After it is read, he asks, "Does anyone have any suggestions on what we can do? Remember, we are just listing ideas, not discussing them yet. This is called brainstorming." Figure 11.1 (see p. 90) shows the information he recorded under the ideas column.

Once he is certain that students have no more ideas, Mr. Lopez asks, "What are the facts that we already know?" He records students' answers in the second column, as shown in Figure 11.2 (see p. 91).

FIGURE 11.1

PBL Chart Showing Student Ideas to Allow All Students to Use the Basketball Area

Ideas	Facts	Learning Issues	Action Plan
One day for the big kids and one day for the little kids. Make another basketball court. Tell the big kids to let the little kids play. Have different lunch periods.			

After all known information has been collected, Mr. Lopez moves students along to the third column, wanting to make sure that it is filled in by the end of the first period. Before the end of the period, he wants to ask students to choose which idea they think is the best solution and to put their initials next to it. To keep the process going, he suggests, "Now, let's look at what we need to find out so we can make some suggestions about this problem." Students' answers fill the third column, as in Figure 11.3 (see p. 92).

The next day Mr. Lopez starts class by reviewing the information in each column: "Let's look at the list of what we need to know and find out who would like to do some work on each." The children take turns reading the list out loud, choosing topics to research from the third column. Some children decide to work by themselves, while others choose to work on larger questions as a group.

When this is complete, Mr. Lopez says, "Now that we have chosen our topics, we need to decide how we can go about finding this information." The children talk about how they could answer their question and what resources are available. During the discussion, Mr. Lopez fills in the fourth column (see Figure 11.4 on p. 93).

FIGURE 11.2

PBL Chart Showing Student Ideas and Facts About Using the Basketball Area

Ideas	Facts	Learning Issues	Action Plan
One day for the big kids and one day for the little kids. Make another basketball court. Tell the big kids to let the little kids play. Have different lunch periods.	Big kids won't let little kids play. Little kids want to play on the basketball court. Basket is very high. There are a lot of kids on the playground. Sometimes there are fights. Have to make suggestions.		

Mr. Lopez has already told the principal, school librarian, and gym teachers to expect visits from his students. He now checks with the people students want to interview to confirm their availability, and he negotiates with teachers of 7th and 8th graders to allow his students to interview theirs. He schedules a third day of work so students can perform their research and collect the information they need.

Once they return from their interviews, Mr. Lopez points out things they still need to discover. He tells the students who have found out the cost of an aide to calculate how much it would cost to hire that person for a school year. He also suggests that students who measured the playground and the basketball court use their measurements to find an area in or near the school big enough to put another basketball court.

Revisiting the Problem

Mr. Lopez asks the children to report on their research. For example, he asks, "John, was the principal able to give you the information you

---

FIGURE 11.3

PBL Chart Showing Student Ideas, Facts, and What Students Think They Should Know About the Basketball Area

Ideas	Facts	Learning Issues	Action Plan
One day for the big kids and one day for the little kids. Make another basketball court. Tell the big kids to let the little kids play. Have different lunch periods.	Big kids won't let little kids play. Little kids want to play on the basketball court. Basket is very high. There are a lot of kids on the playground. Sometimes there are fights. Have to make suggestions.	Can we change lunch hours? How big is the playground? Can we have another court? Can a teacher watch the big kids on the court? Could we use the gym? How many little kids want to play? Why won't the big kids let the little kids play? How much will baskets and balls cost?	

---

needed?" When John answers that the principal couldn't give all the information, Mr. Lopez suggests, "Perhaps Sara's interview with the gym teacher will give us the information you didn't get from the principal." He continues until all the students have the opportunity to evaluate their resources and share their information with the whole class.

Next he suggests, "Let's go back to the ideas that were listed to see if you want to take some off the list or if there are some we want to add. We also want to see if, now that you have done some research, you still think the idea you chose was the best."

FIGURE 11.4

PBL Chart Showing Student Ideas, Facts, What Students Think They Should Know, and Resources to Learn About Using the Basketball Area

Ideas	Facts	Learning Issues	Action Plan
One day for the big kids and one day for the little kids. Make another basketball court. Tell the big kids to let the little kids play. Have different lunch periods.	Big kids won't let little kids play. Little kids want to play on the basketball court. Basket is very high. There are a lot of kids on the playground. Sometimes there are fights. Have to make suggestions.	Can we change lunch hours? How big is the playground? Can we have another court? Can a teacher watch the big kids on the court? Could we use the gym? How many little kids want to play? Why won't the big kids let the little kids play? How much will baskets and balls cost?	Ask the gym teacher how much baskets and balls cost. Ask the little kids how many want to play. Interview big kids about why they won't let little kids play. Measure the playground. Ask the custodian about the size of the playground. Ask principal about changing lunch hour. Ask principal about getting a teacher to watch the playground.

The children go through the list of ideas, giving their reasons why some solutions should be dropped and suggesting new ones. For each of the remaining solutions, Mr. Lopez asks one student to give a reason for adopting the solution and then a reason against adopting that solution. Then the students vote on which solution seems to be most workable in light of the information they have collected.

Mr. Lopez ends the class by saying: "Tomorrow, the principal will be visiting to discuss our recommendations. We need to develop a presentation showing why the school should use our solution."

Producing a Product or Performance

The next day students start by developing ideas for their presentation. Mr. Lopez asks, "How can we convince the principal that our idea is the best thing for the school to do? We need to show that it has many things that are good for the school. These are called advantages. We also need to show that it has very few problems. These are called disadvantages."

On the blackboard he makes a column for advantages and a column for disadvantages. He asks students to fill out both columns, then divides the class into two groups. The larger group works on a way of demonstrating the advantages, while the smaller group works on a way of showing that the few disadvantages are outweighed by the advantages.

Some students color "time-charts" of a proposed schedule showing when older kids would be in the lunchroom and younger students could be on the playground. Other students write down arguments for moving to a two-shift lunch/recess system, which would reduce problems and overcrowding in the lunchroom as well as on the playground. A few students sketch out an idea for a basketball hoop that could be attached to the existing pole at a lower height so that both big and little kids could share the same court.

By the time the principal arrives, students have finished designing their presentation and have rehearsed it once in front of Mr. Lopez.

Evaluating Performance and the Problem

Although the problem did not arise out of the school's curriculum, it provides Mr. Lopez with a vehicle for assessing the performance of a number of students in a variety of areas. He also can observe how students work collaboratively.

Aside from evaluating problem-solving skills, Mr. Lopez can use the assignment to gauge students' skills in math, oral language, writing, and logic. Throughout the assignment, Mr. Lopez scrutinizes his students' performance, especially their ability to see potential solutions, ask the right questions, and find the answers. Then he measures students' ability to work without directions and both to lead and to follow when working in a group. Finally, he evaluates the students on their performance in the final presentation.

12 Making the Shift to Problem-Based Learning

F ollowing are some suggestions for creating an environment that encourages problem-based learning (PBL). Also included are sample problems and resources for solving them as well as a discussion about making the move to problem-based learning.

Space for Active Learning

The room arrangement sets the tone for the class and determines how it will function. A room with desks bolted to the floor facing the teacher and the blackboard speaks volumes about how the class will be run.

The arrangement of the classroom should differ according to the type of teaching used and the behavioral expectations for students. In problem-based learning, the arrangement of furniture, equipment, and resources must allow students to work in organized teams, informal groups, or individually. The room arrangement also must facilitate discussion as well as encourage research, and it may need to change according to each day's activities.

On a day when students will share their thoughts or information, the teacher may want to set up a semicircle facing the blackboard so classmates can talk to each other and still read notes taken by the recorder. When students work in groups, the teacher could clump desks together into workstations. If the teacher brings in research material or other resources, he may want to set up activity areas in different parts of the room.

Teachers should remember that space for active learning is available outside the classroom as well. Students should be able to visit school, public, or university libraries; museums; organizations; and colleges. For some problems, students may need to survey classmates throughout the school or interview adults in the community. Other problems may require students to measure, model, investigate, or create change in places or things outside the school.

Resources for Investigating

Barrows points out that "students in a problem-based learning course do not receive a standard body of information in a defined sequence. . . . It is totally individualized. . . . on the basis of their own self-directed study" (Barrows 1985, p. 49). A PBL classroom, then, should have a variety of materials from which students can choose according to their research plan. If possible, the teacher may want to provide students with multimedia resources including computer programs and CD-ROMs, the Internet, specialty computer networks, television documentaries, and newspaper and magazine microfilms.

The teacher should make additional resources available through research periods in the library or computer room. Additional information might be found through local colleges or universities, museums, research institutes, historical societies, arts organizations, science centers, lobbying groups, advocacy organizations, nonprofit associations, foundations, cultural centers, corporations, and governments.

Elementary school classrooms tend to be self-contained, so PBL encourages elementary teachers to bring in resources from other parts of the school. As students progress through the grades and as they become more and more independent in their learning, they will find their resources in evermore widening circles, both inside and outside the school.

Resources should be specific to the problem. The teacher might consider contacting national or local organizations and businesses that work on issues raised by the problem. If the school has an Internet connection, the teacher can find appropriate Web sites, news groups, and e-mail lists.

The teacher also can identify people in the community who might be willing to share their knowledge of a topic.

Finally, throughout the year, the available resources should be more complex. Students working on their first problem may focus on the textbook or the encyclopedia. In future problems, they could be encouraged, for example, to locate articles through *The Reader's Guide to Periodical Literature* or to contact people in the community.

Time for Solving Problems

The most scarce resource is time. To make the best use of available time for a PBL lesson, teachers should begin their planning well in advance. The summer before school begins is a good time for teachers to review their curriculum, determine where to use PBL, and begin writing their problems. Then, before introducing the problem to the class, the teacher should gather resources so students can find them quickly. In addition, the teacher should speak with adults the students may wish to interview and obtain their permission to be contacted.

Ideally, the PBL unit should be scheduled so that students can work for long periods without being interrupted by a vacation break. While middle and high school teachers are constrained by school schedules and cannot allocate as much time per day as elementary teachers, they can encourage students to perform much of the research and construction of the product after school or during free periods. Instead of assigning specific homework tasks, the teacher may want to develop a schedule for when each stage of the PBL activity should be complete so students can evaluate their progress and decide if they need to find additional time on their own to finish. This further develops students' sense of ownership and responsibility. In addition, since PBL lends itself to interdisciplinary work, two teachers with many of the same students could collaborate on the PBL problem, combining their class periods.

Sample Problems and Possible Resources

Although teachers should bring many resources into the classroom, many problems will require students to perform research on their own in school libraries or outside the school. Teachers, especially in the upper grades, may give their students more freedom to find their own resources in the school and community. In all cases, it is key that the teacher work with the school librarian and notify possible sources to tell them that they may be contacted by students working on a problem.

In general, the teacher should carefully consider the available resources and let them guide the writing of the problem. The teacher also should ask the school librarian and curriculum experts about the materials and resources they know are available. If materials need to be ordered from outside the city, the teacher should request them well in advance. However, instead of just giving students reference materials and lists of people to contact, the teacher also should encourage them to determine their own needs and make their own suggestions about references. Frequently, because of the student-directed nature of PBL, some resources will go unused or students will find others that the teacher did not consider.

Social Studies

> Some people believe that the Underground Railroad never existed or was so secret that people today cannot find it. You have been asked to develop a brochure for a tour company taking students to sites on the Underground Railroad.

This social studies problem would require a number of nonfiction sources, including history texts, books on African American history, books on local history, laws of the pre-Civil War period, religious literature of the time, and historical and contemporary maps. In addition, the teacher might want to make available narratives of the lives of escaped slaves and historical fiction. Sample tourist brochures would provide useful models for students' own brochures.

The teacher could encourage students to contact professors of African American history, museums, and historical societies. With some digging, students may be able to locate and interview families of people whose ancestors escaped slavery through the Underground Railroad. They also may be able to use the Internet to contact people who live in communities along the various Underground Railroad routes.

Mathematics

> Our school library is going to be completely reorganized. Each mathematics class on our grade level has been asked to submit a series of designs for its reorganization. You are asked to submit a model, together with a narrative description.

For this problem on libraries, a teacher would, of course, collect basic supplies such as graphing paper, rulers, scissors, construction paper, glue, contact paper, and chipboard. The teacher also would collect information about different classification systems (Dewey Decimal, Library of Congress), ratios, interior design, and technology. The teacher could find articles on how computers and other information sources are replacing books and traditional library materials.

In addition, students may wish to examine the history of libraries, visit other schools' libraries, interview students about their needs, and talk to architects and librarians about good library design. The teacher might suggest that students contact library supply companies and the American Library Association for additional information.

English as a Second Language

> Our class has indicated that it likes to read poetry. However, no one book or series of books contains a wide enough range of poems, poems on multicultural themes, or authors from a variety of cultures. Our class must come up with a plan to solve this problem.

To work on the above problem, an English as a Second Language (ESL) teacher would need to make available several collections of poems in English simple enough for students to read. The teacher also would offer information on the ESL department's budget, catalogs from poetry publishers, books on the state of poetry in the United States, information on poetry contests, and copies of poetry magazines.

Students could write to poetry anthologists, to poets whose work they like, or to English departments at colleges and universities. Students could talk to professors in departments devoted to specific ethnic groups and foreign literatures. They also could contact the Modern Language Association and poets' organizations.

Health/Science

> With the introduction of the new food pyramid, there has been a great deal of controversy over the change in the school lunch program. Many people want to make lunch more nutritious while others want to return to the old lunch menus. You have been asked to compare the nutritional value and popularity among students of the new and old menus and make a report to the school principal on what changes, if any, should be made.

A science teacher working on this problem would have to alert the school's food service staff, health personnel, school dietician, and assistant principal in charge of the cafeteria that a number of students may attempt to get information from them. In addition, the teacher should collect information on nutrition, contact groups supporting health and nutrition, and request a copy of the cafeteria budget. Besides interviewing adults in the school, students could interview fellow classmates from all grades and observe in the lunchroom to see what food is bought most often.

Science

> Your school wants to save money on its heating costs. It is considering changing to oil heat, but some people object, saying that it will not be as efficient or economical. You have been asked to report to the school board on which energy source—coal, gas, oil, or electricity—would be best.

In this class, the teacher would have to alert the school engineer, maintenance department, and possibly the principal or superintendent of upcoming interviews by students. The teacher also should contact the local energy company for booklets comparing various sources of energy and write for information from environmental organizations and representatives from the oil and gas industries.

Books on energy and how different energy sources produce heat would be useful. Students may want to check the school budget to see how much is currently spent. They also could visit other schools and contact hospitals, colleges, and similar institutions to find out what form of heating they use and its cost.

Elements of a Problem–Based Learning Problem

For many teachers and students, making the shift to PBL may seem to require taking a big risk. In PBL, teachers and students both change their roles. Students work on their own and set their own direction, while the teacher provides guidance and support. Although this is different from traditional teaching, it is very similar to what students will experience in their future employment. Few jobs come with a list of procedures that should be followed in all situations. Employers will expect their workers to perform on their own, think through difficult situations, and find answers to problems. When making the shift to problem-based learning, keep in mind the following important elements of the PBL problem.

Simplicity

The PBL problem cannot tackle everything under the sun or give students unlimited freedom to research anything they like. Instead, teachers must decide on the curriculum area and subject around which they are going to write the problem, clearly define the issue, and narrow its scope. Instead of drawing up a problem on the whole Civil War period, a social studies teacher would create a problem focusing on the Underground Railroad. A science teacher would create a problem on chemical reactions that neutralize upset stomachs, not chemical reactions in general.

Although elementary school teachers have less formal divisions in subjects, they too must craft their PBL problem around clearly defined issues and limit its range. Teachers in self-contained classrooms have myriad options. They can develop a problem in any of the disciplines, create an interdisciplinary problem, or write a problem around an issue that emerges from the day-to-day life of the classroom. However, teachers still must limit their choice to a relatively small area such as a unit on mapping neighborhoods or discovering the games children play in a particular country.

Teachers also should limit the selection of skills students will develop through working on the problem. While every problem will build research and problem-solving skills, teachers should restrain the requirements for producing the final product. Throughout the year, the problems should increase in difficulty. For example, in the first problem the teacher may give the students all the resources needed to solve the problem. By the middle of the year, students could locate their own resources and go beyond the school to track down additional material.

Clarity

Teachers using PBL should be very clear in what they hope to accomplish. It is easy for students to become confused the first few times they use PBL techniques. Unless students thoroughly understand PBL and what they are expected to do, they automatically will revert to traditional patterns and the lesson will not be successful. Therefore, the teacher should have very clear objectives, write a coherent problem statement that will facilitate achieving these objectives, clearly communicate the process, check to make sure students understand the objectives and the process, set high standards and inform students of them, and select products and performances that will allow for evaluating students as well as the PBL process and the teacher's performance with it.

Consistency

Teachers using problem-based learning must be consistent. Students have spent years learning the procedures and expectations of traditional teaching, and they need to develop the same comfort level with PBL strategies. Teachers should explain each stage of the process carefully, telling students not only what they will be doing but how each stage fits into the process and how it will help them solve the problem and produce the final result.

Communication

The first teacher to make the shift to PBL in a school should be prepared to explain PBL and its process not only to the students but also to curious parents, teachers, and administrators who are unfamiliar with this way of teaching. Other teachers using PBL in their classrooms have dealt with this issue by emphasizing how PBL develops students' problem-solving skills and independence *in addition to* furthering their understanding of curriculum, research skills, and work-related skills.

Without criticizing traditional teaching, they explain that students in PBL classes remember more of what they learn, since they were the ones who found the information. Also, they are more enthusiastic about learning, since the problems often emerge out of their own lives or are closely tied to their own experiences. Others have used work-related arguments, saying that in the workplace, employees will not have teachers providing instruction and direction. Students must learn to work on their own and direct their own activities.

References

Albanese, M., and S. Mitchell. (1993). "Problem-Based Learning: A Review of Literature on Its Outcomes and Implementation Issues." *Academic Medicine* 68, 1: 52–81.

Barrows, H.S. (1985). *How to Design a Problem-Based Curriculum for the Preclinical Years.* New York: Springer Publishing Company.

Barrows, H.S. (1994). "Problem-Based Learning." Springfield, Ill.: Problem-Based Learning Institute, mimeo.

Barrows, H.S., and R.H. Tamblyn. (1980). *Problem-Based Learning: An Approach to Medical Education.* New York: Springer Publishing Company.

Board of Education of the City of New York. (1995). *Curriculum Framework: Knowledge, Skills and Abilities Grades PreK–12.* New York City: Author.

Dewey, J. (1916, 1944). *Democracy and Education.* New York: The Free Press.

National Center for Education Statistics. (1996). *Digest of Education Statistics.* Washington, D.C.: U.S. Department of Education, Office of Educational Research and Improvement.

National Council of Teachers of Mathematics. (1994). *Curriculum and Evaluation Standards for School Mathematics.* Reston, Va.: Author.

Problem-Based Learning Institute. (1994). "Problem-Based Learning Sequence." Springfield, Ill.: Author, mimeo.

Sarnoff, A.P. (March 18, 1996). "Hotbed of Innovation." *U.S. News and World Report*, pp. 92–94.

Suggested Readings

Albanese, M., and S. Mitchell. (1993). "Problem-Based Learning: A Review of Literature on Its Outcomes and Implementation Issues." *Academic Medicine* 68, 1: 52–81.

Identifies and discusses PBL issues in the research literature.

Aspy, D.N., C.B. Aspy, and P.M. Quinby. (1993). "What Doctors Can Teach Teachers About Problem-Based Learning." *Educational Leadership* 58, 7: 22–24.

Describes changes taking place in medical schools. Trend toward problem-based learning will eventually have an effect throughout education. Teachers shifting to PBL will need to become adept at listening, dealing with and framing questions, and writing problems.

Barrows, H.S. (1985). *How to Design a Problem-Based Curriculum for the Preclinical Years.* New York: Springer Publishing Company.

Provides the medical educator with a guide for converting to problem-based learning. Introduction is good overview of PBL for the general educator.

Barrows, H.S. (1988). *The Tutorial Process.* Rev. ed. Springfield, Ill.: Southern Illinois University School of Medicine.

A step-by-step manual for the PBL tutor. Good overview of the process for the general educator. Reader need merely replace "tutor" with "teacher."

Barrows, H.S., and R.M. Tamblyn. (1980). *Problem-Based Learning: An Approach to Medical Education.* New York: Springer Publishing Company.

Written with a focus on problem-based learning in medical education. Chapters 1, 6, 10, and 11 should be of particular interest to teachers at all levels. Chapter 1 gives a well-thought rationale for selecting PBL as a teaching tool in medical education, but the reasoning is applicable to all education. Chapter 6 deals with self-directed learning, a key objective for PBL, and Chapter 10 addresses the difficulties encountered in changing over to PBL. Chapter 11 provides an excellent summary of the process of PBL, the process of self-directed learning, and the educational advantages of PBL.

Kaufman, A., ed. (1993). *Implementing Problem-Based Medical Education: Lessons from Successful Innovations.* New York: Springer Publishing Company.

A collection of articles by the faculty of the medical school of the University of New Mexico. Each article reports on findings and makes recommendations. Excellent resource for administrators contemplating use of PBL.

Nooman, Z.M., H.G. Schmidt, and E.S. Ezzat, eds. (1990). *Innovation in Medical Education: An Evaluation of Its Present Status.* New York: Springer Publishing Company.

A collection of articles describing innovations in medical education. Chapters 1 and 2 report on successful PBL innovations at the University of New Mexico and McMaster. Chapter 13 reports on the reactions of staff and students to the introduction of PBL. Important for persons wanting to bring in PBL.

Norman, G.R., and H.G. Schmidt. (1992). "The Psychological Basis of Problem-Based Learning: A Review of the Evidence." *Academic Medicine* 67, 9: 557–565.

Article reviews research evidence related to advantages of problem-based learning.

Pallie, W., and D.H. Carr. (1987). "The McMaster Medical Education Philosophy in Theory, Practice and Historical Perspective." *Medical Teacher* 9, 1: 59–71.

Review of problem-based learning at McMaster Medical School. Provides context for present PBL.

Stepien, W.J., S.A. Gallagher, and D. Workman. (1993). "Problem-Based Learning for Traditional and Interdisciplinary Classrooms." *Journal for the Education of the Gifted* 16, 4: 338–357.

Describes two applications of problem-based learning at the Illinois Mathematics and Science Academy: a senior elective as well as a sophomore-required course. Program effectiveness also is discussed.